HELL ON LAND
DISASTER AT SEA

The Story of
Merrill's Maraude
and the Sinking
of the Rhona

By Fred E. Randle
with the collaboration of
William W. Hughes

TURNER PUBLISHING COMPANY
Paducah, Kentucky

TURNER PUBLISHING COMPANY
Publishers of America's History
412 Broadway
P.O. Box 3101
Paducah, KY 42002-3101
(270) 443-0121

Turner Publishing Company Staff
Editor: Randy Baumgardner
Graphic Design: Tyranny J. Bean

Copyright © 2002 Fred E. Randle
Publishing Rights: Turner Publishing Company.
All rights reserved.

Library of Congress
Control No: 2001098726
ISBN 978-1-63026-956-2

This book or any part thereof may not be reproduced by
any means, mechanical or electronic, without the prior
written consent of FredE. Randle and Turner Publishing
Company. Printed in the United States of America. Additional copies may be purchased from Turner Publishing
Company. Limited Edition.

TABLE OF CONTENTS

FOREWORD

Fred E. Randle survived some of the most perilous and punishing combat action of World War II. Concomitantly, he frequently was at the right place at the right time to witness some of military history's most absorbing events.

He saw the virtual beginning of the Space Age when history's first successful guided missile sunk the HMT Rohna, a British transport carrying more than 2,000 American veterans, some 1,047 of whom died in the waters of the Mediterranean Sea. It was the worst at-sea disaster ever to claim American military victims, the battleship Arizona losing only a few more men while moored in a state of peacetime inertia at Pearl Harbor. Randle was a few hundred feet away on the top deck of the Rohna's sister ship, the Karoa, when a German HS 293 air-to-surface missile struck the Rohna amidships. The incident, long cloaked in secrecy by the American and British governments, occurred several months before the Nazis' first VI and V2 buzz bombs hit London and the Belgian city of Antwerp after it was recaptured by the Allies and became one of their principal supply bases.

But that was only the start of Randle's exceptional wartime experience. His Mediterranean convoy of 12 ships was loaded with at least 30,000 American soldiers en route to the China-Burma-India Theater of Operations in the Great War. Upon arrival there, Randle was assigned to the 5307th Composite Unit (Provisional), later to be known as Merrill's Marauders, surely one of the most heroic infantry regiments in the history of American arms.

Randle and the other men in that regiment had to march some 800 miles over what Winston Churchill described as the world's most forbidding terrain, fighting at least 26 separate engagements against the Japanese along the way. Theirs is the story of warriors who were told by the American high command in Washington (with the concurrent knowledge of Churchill and Franklin D. Roosevelt) that they should expect at least 85 per cent casualties in their unit - a forecast that proved to be dismally accurate. Of an original force of some 3,000 soldiers, less than 300 were still on their feet when the regiment finally captured the strategic Myitkyina airstrip in North Burma, a compacted gravel runway near a village of a few hundred people, yet one which subsequently became the busiest airbase in the entire Allied war effort.

But even the sacrifices in the Marauders' long march and the capture of the airstrip were not enough. A number of those who were wounded or disabled by jungle diseases were flown to a hospital several hundred miles away, only to be forced out of their beds to assist in the capture of the village of Myitkyina itself. This became necessary when the Japanese units in the town had been strongly reinforced as the result of a costly blunder by one of America's most noted generals in the war, Joseph W. (Vinegar Joe) Stilwell. Historians are awakening to the fact that Stilwell, while justifiably heralded for his determination in the war effort, was nevertheless to be more condemned than praised for some of his most important strategic decisions, not to mention his insensitive and, at times, heartless treatment of the men in his command. The story told by Randle in this book is a devastating affirmation of this revisionist history.

Despite its many fascinating aspects, the conflict in Southeast Asia is a relatively 'forgotten war.' Ask most people to name the areas officially designated as major Theaters of Operation in World War II and they will identify only two: The European and Pacific Theaters. Similarly, they will identify only two Supreme Commanders, Dwight D. Eisenhower and Douglas MacArthur. Yet the C-B-I not only was officially designated as a third theater, but also had its own Supreme Commander who was British in his nationality, namely that colorful figure with the arresting name of Lord Louis Mountbatten.

In fact, Mountbatten was given the impressive designation as Supreme Commander of the Southeast Asia Command, which included not only the American forces in the CBI Theater, but also control of a large number of troops from the United Kingdom, Australia, Canada, India, Africa and China, the last named being a country whose control was most important to the Allies in both the Pacific and Asian regions.

Mountbatten was accurately described by his principal biographer (Philip Ziegler) as being "glamorous and almost indecently handsome." He was that and much more. He not only conducted his military command responsibilities quite competently, he later earned a batch of kudos as the Viceroy of India who almost single-handedly brought about that nation's independence, despite the fact that it was accompanied by a violent Hindu-Moslem partition that haunts the subcontinent to this day. Finally, Mountbatten received a good deal of credit for the strengthening of the British navy, both before and after the war. It is therefore quite ironic that most Americans today can identify Mountbatten only as the great uncle of Britain's Prince Charles who adored him more than any other male figure in the prince's life. Charles, in fact, was so devastated by Mountbatten's assassination by Irish terrorists that the prince's friends say it was a long time before he recovered emotionally from that tragedy in his personal life.

But Mountbatten was only one of the most impressive members in the cast of characters involved in the Southeast Asia Command of World War II. He was a man whose leadership impacted heavily on Merrill's Marauders as a group and on Randle as a commendable member of that outfit. Indeed, it would be hard to find in world history a specific place and time which held the attention or featured the activity of so many imposing leaders, all of them constantly interacting with one another and with the challenging situations facing them.

It starts with Roosevelt and Churchill.

Those two giants in the story of World War II held one of their famed conferences at Quebec in August of 1942 at which they discussed their problems with China's Generalissimo Chiang Kai-Shek and his stormy relationship with General Stilwell. But much of the meeting also was taken up with the problem of how to open the Burma Road in order to augment air transport in the movement of supplies into China, an endeavor which was essential to keep China in the war against its Japanese invaders.

Enter at this point the colorful, mysterious, and altogether fascinating personage of Brigadier General Orde C. Wingate, the originator of "long range penetration" groups. His brigade of "Chindits" proved to be the forerunner of such units as the Office of Strategic Services (O.S.S.), an American intelligence and fighting team which also operated behind the Japanese lines in Burma and which, in turn, was the predecessor of today's Central Intelligence Agency (CIA). The Marauders themselves adopted some of Wingate's tactics, as did the Green Berets who operated so dramatically behind enemy lines in the Vietnam War.

Wingate was such an eccentric character that he once appeared naked in a pep talk to some of his troops. When Great Britain was helping Ethiopia in its war against Italian invaders he lit fires under obstinate camels to make them move forward in the Ethiopian desert.

Later, he suffered such deep bouts of depression that he tried to commit suicide. But, his reputation as a strategist and tactician was so impressive that the British army not only kept him on its roster, but also gave him a tough responsibility in World War II. After he regained his mental balance, the British high command sent him to India to help Stilwell in his plans to recapture northern Burma from the Japanese.

After his arrival, Wingate took a force of about 3,000 British and Gurkha soldiers on a 200-mile foray into western Burma. His mission was never clear and the only accomplishments by his so-called "Chindits" were the blowing of a few bridges and cutting the road to Myitkyina, not anything more than an American O.S.S. detachment had accomplished earlier with a few Yanks and a handful of friendly Kachin tribesmen.

But Churchill was impressed because Wingate was one of only two British generals in Asia who had shown any desire to take the offensive against the Japs, the other being General William J. Slim whose British and Indian troops eventually defeated a large Japanese army in the south of Burma. Consequently, Churchill decided to invite Wingate to the Quebec conference along with Mountbatten. Others in attendance were American Air Corps General Hap Arnold and a number of lesser military figures. All of them were stunned when Wingate made an extremely forceful and charismatic appearance, which Arnold later described in these words: "You took one look at that face, the face of an Indian chieftain, topping a uniform still smelling of jungle and sweat and war, and you thought: 'Hell, this man is serious.' And when he began to talk you found out just how serious!"

Needless to say, FDR also was impressed, and he and Churchill decided that Wingate's Chindit force ought to be augmented by some American soldiers who would strike deep into north Burma to capture Myitkyina and its strategic airstrip. And it was in that way that the formation of the regiment later to be known as Merrill's Marauders was conceived and put into action.

As it turned out, Wingate did not get to control the regiment. Stilwell later insisted that an American regiment ought to be under American command, and he thus persuaded Chief of Staff George C. Marshall to spirit the Marauders away from Wingate but, not without Wingate's anticipated negative reaction. He told one of Stilwell's staff members that Vinegar Joe "can take his Americans and stick them up his ass."

Some weeks later, however, Wingate proved he was a team player when he took his Chindits deep into Burma to help the Marauders and lost his life in the effort. Before he died in a tragic plane crash he accomplished a feat unparalleled in military history. He loaded hundreds of men and mules onto gliders and landed them far behind Japanese lines to again cut strategic railroads and destroy a number of enemy installations.

Two other charismatic figures in the CBI Theater were aviators who conducted their work in the grand style. One of them was General Claire Chennault, originally the founder of the famous prewar Flying Tigers and later named the commanding general of the Fourteenth Air Force. His military exploits were commendable but his strategic judgments left much to be desired.

The other famous aviator was none other than Colonel Phillip Cochran, the fearless flyer who helped Wingate in his second mission by providing the planes and pilots to pull Wingate's gliders. Cochran was also the dashing American pilot who was dramatized as "Flip" Corkin in the famous Milton Caniff comic strip "Terry and the Pirates."

Among still other important personages were the political leaders of India and China, Mohandas K. Gandhi and Chiang Kai-Shek. Gandhi, of course, is regarded by many savants as one of the most admirable social and political figures in the history of the world, and deservedly so. However, he was a controversial figure to the western world during the war and allied officers and soldiers in the CBI Theater did not hold him in high regard. He had even been an Adolph Hitler admirer prior to the war, although he later changed his views toward the Nazi tyrant. More importantly, his massive demonstrations in his passive resistance to the British Raj, as meritorious as they no doubt were, could not be tolerated during the war. This was at a time when Indian soldiers were being drafted into the Allied forces to hold back the Japanese invaders of Southeast Asia, the Japs at one point crossing the Burma border into India and capturing several towns in the Imphal area. Consequently, in view of Gandhi's pacifist views and his disruptive activities, the British decided his initiatives were too great a distraction to the war effort, and decided to keep him in prison until the war ended. This decision was not compatible with Western ideals of political and social justice, but it may have been necessary in view of the war's already formidable complications.

Chiang Kai-Shek was a different cup of Asian tea. Despite the glaring deficiencies in General Stilwell's character and diplomatic skills, he did not deserve the inimical actions taken against him by Chiang and his powerful wife, known to the world as "Madam Chiang." Nor was Stilwell alone in being forced to deal with Chiang's constant insistence that the war in Burma take second place to his defense against the Japanese who had already occupied eastern China. FDR and Churchill joined Stilwell in trying to keep Chiang on track with respect to the Allied plan to take Burma as a necessary step in giving Chiang the assistance he needed, assistance which first required a land route for men and supplies into western China.

Nevertheless, Stilwell, who spoke the Chinese language fluently, finally persuaded Chiang to give him two Chinese divisions in the drive to sweep Japanese forces out of northern Burma. While he hated Chiang, Stilwell held a high regard for the potential of properly trained Chinese troops in combat situations, an assessment which later was to be confirmed in some but not all of the Chinese activity in Burma.

But Stilwell also had his failings, and they were numerous and severe. Randle covers these deficiencies in detail as he traces the general's supervision of the military endeavors of Merrill's Marauders.

In any event, the strategy confirmed at the Quebec conference was as follows:

The Southeast Asia Command was established with the understanding that the British, with the help of their Indian divisions, would move into southwest Burma and then push on east to free the country's principal cities of Mandalay and Rangoon.

Meanwhile, Stilwell and his Americans would continue their building of the Ledo Road to connect with the famed old Burma Road in east-central Burma. Concomitantly, since the road construction already was making progress in India's Assam Province, Merrill's Marauders, with the help of Chinese soldiers, would proceed down the completed part of the road which, by the time the Marauders started their march, had reached a point near Taipah Ga in the Patkai Mountains between Assam and Burma.

From that point on, the road builders would have to follow the advance of the Marauders, rather than the other way around.

All told, this meant that the Marauders, already having traversed more than two hundred miles, would then have to march another 600 miles over narrow and rough trails, through jungles and across mountains in order to achieve the objective of capturing Myitkyina which had been kept secret by Stilwell.

Meanwhile, the American air corps was to embark on the greatest airlift in history, flying many thousands of tons of supplies and weapons to Chiang Kai-Shek's western China headquarters and distribution center at Kunming. This "over-the-hump" activity across the Himalayans, the world's highest and most treacherous mountains for flying operations, subsequently became world famous, and justifiably so. The C-47 Dakotas or "Goony Birds" proved to be such great aircraft in that endeavor that they eventually were converted into the famous DC-3s, the planes which raised post-war American commercial aviation to a new level of service. Similarly, the completion of the 500 miles of the Ledo Road was certainly the greatest military construction project in the history of mankind.

In the face of all the background material presented above, it should be said that the book you are about to read is not concerned as much with great leaders and grand strategies as it is with the experiences and viewpoints of an individual soldier who fought and suffered for the causes of democracy in the Burma war. Too often the soldier himself and his contributions to victory are forgotten in the hyperbolic praises heaped upon generals and political leaders by many historians. This is not the case with this narrative, and consequently, its interest is greatly enhanced for the reader who wants to know what war really is like.

Fred E. Randle will tell you exactly what it is like and you will never forget it.

WILLIAM W. HUGHES

Prelude To War

I thought it was strange when Jude never brayed.

He surely wasn't like any mule I had worked with back in Missouri where I was born. But he was big and strong and not as stubborn as I knew Missouri mules to be.

Then I found out why Jude was so amiable. He had been through a United States army basic training course at Fort Bliss, Texas for jungle duty against the Japanese. That meant that his voice box had to be surgically removed to be sure he made no sound as we embarked on our long and arduous trek in northeast India and northwest Burma. Which made a lot of sense in the Burma jungle where, as I was soon to learn, we could stumble upon some of our enemies around any of the numerous curves in trails which snaked through dense forests and thick underbrush.

That training course did some other fine things for Jude. He became obedient and, despite the exceptionally heavy load he had to carry, usually followed docilely along when I tugged him forward. He also was trained not to buck or even shudder when he heard gunfire, no matter how close. I'll talk more about Jude later, and how I was able to survive, even if he wasn't, during our exceptionally dangerous mission against our Japanese foes. First a word about how I found myself in a predicament which, in retrospect, I could have and perhaps should have avoided.

It all began when I became a volunteer in a gamble so foolish that it made a drunken Las Vegas high roller look like a paragon of profundity.

My buddy, Seymour Schoenfeld, and I were suffering in the 110 degree heat in the so-called Tent City near Calcutta, India, where a large contingent of newly-arrived American soldiers was being sorted out for different kinds of duties in an area recently designated as the China-Burma-India Theater of Operations. One day a sergeant gathered an unsuspecting group of us together to talk enticingly to us about a way we could avoid any further boredom in the repugnant location where we were then situated. It was particularly repelling because the year was 1943 and Calcutta and Bengal Province were suffering from one of the worst famines in the 20th Century. More than a million people had died by the time we arrived there, and it was difficult to determine whether there were more victims in Calcutta or in the city's surrounding countryside.

One thing we did know was that it was not advisable to accept a weekend pass to visit the city. History already had determined that Calcutta was one of this planet's largest concentrations of people with serious contagious diseases, and the famine had made the metropolis even more desolate and more forbidding. The city's main street, Chowringhee Road, presented a scene that eclipsed any imaginative vision of the torments of hell. Literally hundreds of bodies lay along the sides of the thoroughfare and often out in the center of it. Many of the victims were women and children who had been reduced to little more than skeletons, even before their demise. Hordes of vultures tore away at the mass of hideous corpses which emitted an overpowering stench. American soldiers who drove jeeps down Chowringhee were so repelled and angered by the sight that they frequently swerved their vehicles into the vulture flocks and shook their fists in triumph as the flesh and feathers of the repulsive birds disintegrated into the already contaminated air of the city.

Processions of Hindu relatives of victims of the famine could be seen every day as they carried the bodies of the deceased on crude litters to their final destination on the burning ghats on the banks of the Hooghly River which flowed through the city. Most of the soldiers at Tent City experienced typical American curiosity and decided to visit the ghats, only to wish later that they had resisted their morbid impulses. I was one of them. Equally disturbing were the nighttime funeral processions which moved slowly down Chowringhee Road, while the pallbearers illumined the scene with the candles they held while they marched toward their dismal destination.

So I listened and listened carefully when that sergeant at Tent City told all of us how we could escape the undesirable environment in which we then found ourselves. It was easy, the sergeant said. All we had to do was join a new detachment of soldiers who were going to embark on a secret venture. Yes, he did acknowledge that it was going to be "dangerous" and "hazardous", two synonyms that should have warned me off the sergeant's proposal. But he told us that chances for survival were reasonably good and there was one big enticement: everyone who joined the enterprise was to be given an alluring guarantee — that the assignment would last no longer than ninety days and, at the end of that period, we would be rotated back to the United States, a homeland that looked more like heaven to me every day I woke up and found myself in India.

Consequently, I went over the proposition with Schoenfeld and, in the most disastrous action I ever took, I talked both him and myself into accepting that nice little sergeant's proposal. (The sergeant, of course, wisely never joined the mission himself.)

It was to Schoenfeld's admirable credit that he never held my persuasiveness against me. Instead, we remained the best of buddies during the incredible hardships we were to endure, and our friendship deepened to the extent that we remained close buddies until he died many years after the war ended. Our compatibility was surprising in the light of our respective backgrounds. Schoenfeld was a tough and streetwise urban kid who helped his dad sell fruit from a cart on the sidewalks of New York. It was the only way both of them could survive the years of the Great Depression. Like Schoenfeld, I also had to learn the art of economic survival during those same years, but I did it by helping my own father till the soil in the poverty-stricken Ozark hills of Southern Missouri. My own family consumed what inadequate amount of food we raised on our small farm.

Both Schoenfeld and I, in our childhood years, were typical members of Tom Brokaw's "Greatest Generation." Consequently, we were both reared in environments which instilled in us the all-purpose toughness that would help us survive in an unprecedented kind of warfare, a mode of combat which tested the outermost limits of a man's mental and physical endurance.

I was still in high school when the Japanese attack on Pearl Harbor occurred. Moreover, my family's hardscrabble existence was so severe that we didn't even own a radio set in the days when no one had yet dreamed of an invention called television. Consequently, I didn't learn about the Pearl Harbor attack until I went to school on the Monday morning of December 8, 1941. Nor was I unduly concerned about my possible involvement in a war. I had no thought of enlisting and I was determined to finish high school for what seemed to me to be a good reason: I intended to become what available genealogical records indicated would be the first member of my Randle clan ever to finish high school. With that goal achieved, I decided to get a job that would help the war effort. I found one with a Kansas City contractor who was building a manufacturing complex for the production of ammunition powder. Because of the nature of my employment, I again thought that I would not be directly involved in the war. But, I was mistaken. My job lasted only until, at the tender age of 18, I received my draft notice and went home to Mountain View, Missouri, to be inducted.

My orders were to report to Jefferson Barracks in St. Louis where draftees were being sent for assignment to various army bases throughout the country. I thought I was reasonably lucky when I learned I was being sent to Fort Knox, Kentucky, which had a generally good reputation among the nation's military posts, not to mention its stature as the custodian of the nation's gold supplies. Never mind that I would never gain access to this treasure, the very thought of being close to it was intriguing. Moreover, I found on my arrival that Fort Knox was a tough training ground for American soldiers; training that was as thorough as it was efficient for many kinds of combat.

I was initiated into such activities as long night marches and the use and maintenance of a wide variety of weapons. We also were trained to operate all kinds of army vehicles over rough terrain, including half-tracks, tanks, heavy trucks and, of course, the versatile jeep. I later was to become very grateful for the thoroughness of this preparation. This happened when I finally became a participant in a kind of human activity which the base when we completed our training. "War," he said, "is a killing game. You've got to kill or be killed." I later learned the impeccable accuracy of that definition.

Subsequently, after a brief and emotional furlough with my family in Missouri, I was selected in a group of soldiers to be sent to Fort Meade in Maryland for advanced training in the armored field. I never became engaged in armored warfare, but I doubtless needed the further tests of my endurance and physical adaptation to the demands of war which were provided at Meade, including the omnipresent obstacle courses we had to negotiate.

Then came the shocker. On the morning of October 1, 1943, a group of 25 of us trainees was called together for a briefing on special orders dispatching us to a secret destination, the identity of which we would not learn until we arrived there. Little did we know that the trip itself was to become highly eventful.

THE SINKING OF THE ROHNA

It all began when we boarded a train for Newport News, Virginia, and then embarked on a boat which became a small part of a 110-ship convoy crossing the Atlantic Ocean. Our ship was the Booker T. Washington, named for the noted 19th Century Civil Rights leader. Some 500 men and a number of pieces of equipment were crowded into our vessel and we sailed out to sea on October 4, 1943. It was an interesting voyage. We used salt water for showering and many of us succumbed to the anticipated cases of seasickness as our ship tossed and rolled on the turbulent Atlantic waves.

However, our voyage was not without its brighter moments. Porpoises swam alongside our ship, occasionally leaping playfully out of the water. Sunrises and sunsets were spectacular parts of the seascape. Camaraderie aboard ship was strong and many (excluding my wiser self) engaged in high stakes poker and crap games. Moreover, several nighttime storms helped to relieve our boredom and kept the crews busy in securing and tying down equipment before heavy winds and high waves buffeted our ships. And always we indulged in wide ranging speculation on our destination. We watched the destroyers that were escorting our troopships; and we wondered with some uneasiness where we were heading and what we would be doing at the conclusion of our voyage.

Our anxiety grew when, after an 18-day crossing of the Atlantic, we entered the Mediterranean Sea where battleships and destroyers milled about in the vicinity of the convoy. However, things remained calm and uneventful as we moved past the Rock of Gibraltar and eventually docked at Oran, a city of several hundred thousand people on the low plains along the northern coast of Algeria. After debarking from our ships we were sent to an American training camp and subjected once again to rigorous activities, including the inevitable long marches and tough obstacle courses. We also received instruction on how to protect ourselves and our belongings from Algerian thieves who periodically stole into the camp at night.

At the end of a month at Oran, I was among 1,800 Americans who boarded a British troopship, the HMT Karoa, bound eastward to the Suez Canal in a small convoy of about 12 vessels. The ship, built in 1928 and taken out of mothballs for service in the war, was in deplorable condition. It was a wooden, coal-burning vessel with long streaks of rust on its steel hulls. It was armed inadequately, mainly with a few 50-caliber machine guns. Its few lifeboats were in such disrepair that they were inoperable.

Conditions aboard at least one of the other ships in the convoy were just as bad. It was the Rohna, a somewhat larger vessel with more than 2,300 people aboard which sailed near enough to us that we usually could see the American soldiers on deck, wave to them, and even on occasion shout out salutations to them. But on both ships, the crew members received no training on the firing of guns or the lowering of lifeboats. In fact, the combat readiness on the two vessels was so bad that one of my companions on the Karoa worried about a possible engagement with any enemy ship on the grounds that "It would be like shooting water pistols at Al Capone's gang." The Karoa was destined to reach its final destination, but the Rohna was not. Instead, the Rohna was to become the victim of one of the two worst disasters in the history of American naval warfare.

On our second day out of Oran, sailing northeast on the Mediterranean Sea, I was in the hold of our ship when two waves of German bombers appeared and spewed conventional bombs among the boats in our convoy. This was very bad news, as the Mediterranean was known as a "shooting gallery" in 1943 for German planes stationed in Southern France. Indeed, it was called 'Suicide Alley' because the troopships the bombers preyed on usually were not escorted either by allied battleships or air cover, and thus were easy marks for hostile aircraft. This was the case with our own ships and both the Rohna and the Koroa were near the front and outside edge of our convoy, a position which placed them in a vulnerable situation.

As soon as the bombers swept into sight, the commanders on the Rohna and Karoa issued sharply divergent orders to protect the troops on their ships. On the Rohna, Australian Captain T. J. Murphy ordered most of his men below. On the Karoa, the captain ordered all of us to the top deck on the presumption that we would be safer from bomb hits if we scattered ourselves out in the open, which we could not do if we were in the hold. Additionally, we would be in much better position to abandon ship if we needed to.

Sadly and ironically, the captain on the ship which was not bombed, with fewer men aboard, made the right decision and the captain on the ship that was hit, with more men aboard, made the wrong choice. As a result, I was not alone among the men on the Karoa who later suffered twinges of conscience and feelings of guilt when we wondered why we were selected to live and more than a thousand of the men on the Rohna were targeted to die.

When I went topside, I stood at the rail of the Karoa and saw a wave of bombers approaching from the north. At first, the enemy airplanes looked like small specks in the sky, which steadily became larger as the planes moved closer to us. Then my comrades on the deck and I noticed some strange things about the aircraft. Some of them were ejecting what appeared to be other airplanes with very small wings on them. And, as these objects started smashing into the water between the ships in the convoy, we suddenly realized we were experiencing an unusual moment. It wasn't until years later, when spacecraft became a reality in Russia and America, that we realized how historic that moment was. We were seeing something that people outside of a few in Germany had never witnessed before — some airborne vehicles which were not airplanes and which appeared to be guided toward their targets, never mind that they missed all but one of them. We knew they were missiles and not bombs because they were not falling in a vertical drop, but rather were gliding objects which sloped toward their targets. And one of them did hit its target and forever changed man's ventures above the earth. What we saw, of course, were guided missiles and the first really successful use of them in world history. That event occurred when one of the missiles struck the Rohna amidships and literally tore a hole completely through the vessel.

I confess I still suffer nightmares about the devastating havoc the explosion created on the Rohna. Bodies, timbers from the ship, and everything on board were blown high into the air in one hideous mass. The vessel disintegrated to the extent that none of us on the Karoa believed anyone on our sister ship could have survived.

Our British captain then changed his earlier order and yelled at all of us to go below. Which we did and where we huddled in terror and wonderment at what we had seen and heard. At least we were saved the even greater feelings of guilt which we would have suffered in later years if we had seen the tragic aftermath of the missile strike. We were spared the sight of hundreds of bodies of American soldiers floating on the Mediterranean. We also were spared the knowledge, until years later, that some of the ships in the convoy, which could have saved a number of the survivors of the explosion, were ordered instead to steam ahead and not pick any of them up. And the ships unconscionably did that very thing.

However, five ships in the convoy had previously been designated as rescue ships, and one of them, an American minesweeper named the Pioneer, successfully picked up more than 600 of the approximately 1,000 men eventually saved, a little less than half the number who were aboard the Rohna. Another of the rescue ships, the British-owned Holcomb, rescued a very good friend of mine who, like me, later served in the China-Burma-India Theater where the convoy ships were headed at the time of the attack. His name is Eugene Breedlove and he is one of two men still living who have given dramatic accounts of their experiences to me, the other being Kermit (Tony) Brushur.

Both men repressed their tortured memories of the disaster for many years and Breedlove was the first to break his silence. Initially, he gave some statements requested by several writers, including Carlton Jackson, author of the book "Forgotten Tragedy ... the Sinking of the Rohna." Later, Breedlove also submitted, to a tape-recorded interview with the author of this book. The result of that interview was a dramatic account of the tragedy, which now appears here in its entirety:

"Friday, on November 26, 1943, was a gray cloudy day and the morning was the same usual routine with the same breakfast as the preceding day. The troops were finding things to do, such as playing cards, reading books, bull sessions, the usual crap games, and we all wondered where we were going.

"About 3:30 p.m. we were alerted about an air raid by the Germans. The bombers came in three waves and dropped bombs on the whole convoy. They never hit any of the ships, but it was noticeable that they seemed to pick on our ship more than any of the others. Very likely they knew that there were nearly two thousand fresh American troops on board. We had a lot of near misses, which rocked the ship back and forth.

"But the bombers eventually left and everything seemed calm again. I was notified to go to the nose of the ship and stand guard in the "brig" which was on the first floor below deck.

"The only person I had to guard was a lone soldier who had too much to drink and was in there to sober up from the British-supplied rum he had obtained on the ship. I had been on guard only about twenty minutes when the air raid alert sounded again. Very shortly the Officer of the Day came into the brig and ordered me and the prisoner to return to our outfits on the ship.

"I was on the main deck walking toward the main door and I stopped to look at the air raid activity. The cannon in the nose of the ship was again firing and all the convoy ships were taking evasive action. Looking off the left front of the ship, I thought I saw a fighter plane coming down afire and heading toward our ship. About that time I heard someone shout 'Get below soldier,' and I turned to do as I was ordered.

"As I was entering the door, this object hit us amidships. The whole ship seemed to jump when it hit. The early evening lights went out and smoke seemed to be everywhere. Although the soldiers didn't seem to panic you could hear the screams of the men who were injured.

"Almost immediately, the orders were given to abandon ship and the men poured out onto the deck. The ship was beginning to list and I knew I had to get off it as quick as I could. But when I tried to find a lifeboat the facts of life weren't very good. All the lifeboats were rusted in place and couldn't be moved. I saw only one boat being lowered and it was filled with Indian crewmen; and before it reached water, it turned over and spilled all of them (the Indians) into the sea.

"By this time, rope nets had been thrown over the side and men were climbing down the side of the ship into the sea. I had always been instructed that, if I had to abandon ship, I should take some food with me. I was wearing a field jacket over a wool dress uniform and from somewhere I grabbed four cans of "C" rations and crammed them into my jacket pockets.

"I inflated the life jacket with its C02 canisters and let myself into the water. I didn't feel any panic or fear, but the water was very cold and I was glad to have some wool clothes on.

"As soon as I was in the sea, I decided that swimming with GI shoes on was impossible, so taking the shoes off was my next job. The left one came off easily, but a knot in the shoelace of the right shoe stopped this, so I ended up with one shoe on and the other off. And the four cans of 'C' rations were heavy so they were the next to go.

"We were near enough to shore to see the land and I tried swimming toward it. But the tide was going out and it didn't take long to figure out that this was the wrong thing to do. I realized that conserving my strength against the five and six foot waves was necessary, so I put my back to the waves and rode the waves as best I could. Getting away from the ship as quickly as possible was essential and so the tide sweeping me out to sea had its advantages. By now there were men in the water everywhere and it was beginning to get dark.

"In the dusk the German planes were trying to strafe us survivors in the water. The Indian crewmen had on standard 'Mae West' lifejackets, which were equipped with red electric lights. They would turn these lights on and the Germans would strafe the illuminated area. The GIs in the water began telling the Indians to turn the lights off but they were in such a state of fear that they refused to listen.

"As the last of the convoy was passing us an American cruiser slowed down and by loudspeaker someone on it shouted:

'I'm sorry soldiers, but we have been ordered not to stop and pick up survivors. We wish you all good luck!'

"This was the first time I had a sinking feeling because the Rhona was burning and we now were all alone at nightfall in a very big body of water. I don't imagine any survivor will ever forget watching the Rhona as its rear section slid under water while the nose was sticking straight up into the air. Then the nose slowly sunk out of sight.

"A group of more than thirty of us decided to form a circle and hold hands so that we would be seen easier if help came. But, the cold, rough sea began to take its toll. Some of the men would slip silently into the water and were gone while some would fight the water until they were exhausted and then disappear. There was a buck sergeant from Texas who was trying to be our cheerleader. He would try anything he could think of to keep our spirits up. Finally, he said "I'm completely give out and can't go on any longer," and he dropped out of sight. A Jewish boy next to me was so scared he went berserk and started screaming for his mother. Finally, he unbuckled his life belt and he also sank from sight.

"After an hour or two I noticed one of the sections of my life belt was losing air and I began blowing it up. By then there were dead bodies floating all around us. My reasoning was that their life preservers weren't helping them so I took two of theirs and used them the rest of the night.

"At different times, as the night wore on, our dwindling group could see lights of rescue boats in the distance but we couldn't get their attention. As the time passed, the cold water caused our body temperatures to lower, so we tried moving our arms and legs to get the circulation going. That tired us more so we had to stop it.

Later, I was told it was about 2 a.m., we saw a searchlight moving in our direction. It turned out it was on a whaling boat from the British Corvette H.M.S. Holcombe. This time they heard our calls and found us.

"I will always remember the British sailor on the boat telling me to 'Climb aboard, Mate,' and my trying to get in the boat. But there was no strength left. So they grabbed me under my arms and lifted me bodily aboard. I lay in the bottom of the boat unable to move and when we arrived at the ship they had to carry me aboard.

"They immediately took me to the engine room, stripped my clothes off, and placed bottles of hot water between my legs and under my armpits. Then they wrapped me in blankets, and warmth began to return to my body. Needless to say, it wasn't long until I was asleep.

"The next thing I knew, we were docked at some port in North Africa, the name of which I never learned, and we were told that British authorities were there to take care of us. My clothes had disappeared and the only things I had to wear were two pieces of long underwear tops. The sailors gave me my bill-fold and I used the tops as shirt and pants and off the ship I walked.

"Clothes were the least of my worries. It was the dry land that looked so good. The North African native people thought I looked hilarious, but some of them irritated me. They were German sympathizers and they hollered at us: 'Me Nazi, Heil Hitler.'

"I asked the British sailors how many of my group they were able to pick up and they said there were five. So we must have lost at least 25. They also said we were about twenty miles from the bombing when we were picked up. The tide had swept us that distance. Those sailors will always have a warm place in my heart because of their sincerity and helpfulness when it was needed. After leaving the ship, our little group was put in a British lorry and we soon arrived at a British camp and were issued British army uniforms as temporary clothing.

"Oddly enough, by the time we were on land I was feeling pretty good and only had a slight cold as an aftereffect.

"In the afternoon, we were moved to an American camp where more of the survivors had been taken. They weren't prepared to take care of us, but they put all of us in a huge tent and gave us two blankets each with a promise to do better.

"Sleep that night was impossible because there were too many still reliving our experiences in the water and their nightmares kept us awake.

"The next day, Sunday, we had a church service and you can bet there weren't any atheists in our group. We all knew it wasn't just luck that pulled us through this one, and so everyone attended the service.

"The following day was Monday, November 29, and I celebrated my 21st birthday.

"Now, wasn't that a good way to enter adulthood?"

Tony Busher's account of the tragedy is just as stunning as Breedlove's. Like Breedlove, he kept silent for many years about his experiences. Even his wife and children were kept in the dark and Bushur explained that he always felt that he could open up only to someone else who was present at the sinking of the Rohna. Bushur simply finds his memories of his experiences in the Mediterranean so painful that he detests water to this day and even refuses to go to a beach near his home in Florida. And his psychological aversion to water is perfectly understandable when you learn that he spent 13 hours in the sea that dark night after the Rohna went down, five hours more than did Breedlove. Moreover, Bushur had only one man for company during the entire night, the two of them clinging to some floating wreckage from the ship. To have been alone with only one other man in a vast sea of water in the dark of night for so long a time was understandably a nightmarish experience.

Like most people, Bushur had a terrible fear of sharks and every time a fish nipped him in the water it "scared the hell out of me." Since then he has been informed that there never have been any sharks in the Mediterranean. But, this information came much too late to ease his fears when he was floating nearly helpless in the sea.

There also is a poignant footnote to Bushur's story. After the missile struck the Rohna he wisely stayed on deck and refused to go below upon the orders of the captain. This undoubtedly saved his life and he immediately searched for his best buddy, a man named Ed Truckenbroadt. He saw him below deck and tried to throw a rope to him. But the fire from the explosion of the missile made a blazing inferno of the stairs leading to the top deck and Bushur finally saw the futility of his efforts. He then jumped overboard to save himself and found the piece of timber, which kept him afloat.

Bushur, understandably, thought Truckenbroadt had died in the bombing but he wanted to make sure. He had the address of Truckenbroadt's parents in Chicago and he wrote them a letter after Bushur arrived in the CBI Theater. By, return mail he learned that Truckenbroadt survived the bombing even though he had been badly burned. Moreover, they said Truckenbroadt was kept in service and was sent to India. But Bushur never was able to locate him and to this day has not been able to communicate with him about the terrifying experience they shared.

The sinking of the Rohna was not the only unpleasant experience Bushur went through during the war. After he arrived in Burma for service with the Marauders he was so badly wounded by machine gun fire that he nearly lost a leg. However, as horrifying as the Marauders' experiences turned out to be, Bushur thinks his ordeal in the Rohna sinking was worse, and for an interesting reason.

"At least I had a chance (in Burma) to fire back at the enemy and had control of my own actions and could, in a manner of speaking, be responsible for my own life." He also was grateful to be in the hot climate in Burma even if it was a miserable experience. At least it wasn't in some extremely cold climate, Bushur explained, his aversion to it being so strong that he made sure he retired in Florida after his post-war working career. Like Breedlove and myself, Bushur thinks the conditions aboard the British ships in the convoy, including the Rohna and the Karoa, were deplorable.

A MYSTIFYING CONCEALMENT

The aftermath of the sinking of the Rohna was puzzling in many ways.

First, the United States and British governments went to great lengths to conceal the bombing. Immediately after the event there was little or no publicity about it in the press of either of the two countries, despite the fact that it was the worst at-sea maritime disaster in American history. The Pearl Harbor sinking of the Arizona killed 1,015 Americans compared with 1,003 on the Rohna, a difference of only 12 victims, but the Arizona was moored at Pearl Harbor while the Rohna was actually sailing at sea when the two catastrophic attacks occurred. Moreover, the crew and the military passengers on the Rohna were alerted to the possibility of an enemy attack and still fell victim to one, against which it had no defense.

In any event, the sinking of the Rohna has to stand as one of the two worst hostile actions ever taken against ships with American personnel aboard them in World War II. Indeed, it is one of the two worst in the entire naval history of the United States. But, it wasn't until the 1960's that the American government officially released some details on the Rohna incident. In fact, the initial reports from the two governments in the 1940's said that damage to the Rohna had been "negligible." Not even survivors were notified of the deaths of their relatives on the Rohna until years after the disaster. And, one of them did not get the news until 1993 when one Anita Guidry learned that her brother was one of the men on the Rohna, even though he had long been listed only as missing in action.

Why were the two governments so secretive about the incident? They certainly had not been so secretive about Pearl Harbor.

The governments themselves have never tried to explain it. Which, of course, raises more questions as to why such care was taken to withhold information. The most commonly advanced speculation was that America and Great Britain wanted to conceal the fact that Germany had perfected such an advanced new weapon as the guided missile. But if that were true, why didn't the secrecy mandate end when the buzz bombs started hitting London? For this reason alone and many others that explanation simply does not seem plausible.

To this writer, a man who actually witnessed the event, the explanation is much more obvious. Analysts have to understand the condition of the British ships and the incompetence of their British crews in order also to understand why the secrecy wrap was imposed.

Both the Rohna and the Karoa were ships which were built in the 1920's. They not only were old but they were in such deplorable condition that most of an already insufficient number of lifeboats simply were not operable. (The reader should note that only a few, if any lives were saved by the use of these boats.) It was widely assumed that both the Rohna and the Karoa were taken out of mothballs to be pressed into service in the war. Which was perhaps commendable, since the need for troopships to cross the Atlantic and the Mediterranean, not to mention the Pacific, was urgent to say the least. But no effort had been made by the British to restore the ships and particularly none to restore the lifeboats. Most of them were rusted and leaky and very few could have been used. Equally as unpardonable was the British failure to conduct adequate lifesaving drills on board both ships prior to the missile attack. One very perfunctory drill was conducted aboard the Rohna in the Oran harbor, and that was it.

It is also hard to understand why our ships' captains kept the vessels so close together in the convoy, thus making us easier marks for the German bombers. But, conversely, it is also hard to understand how the Germans could have sunk only one of our boats when they were packed that closely on the sea.

In any event, it is my opinion, and I shall never revise it, that Winston Churchill and the British government did not want details of the sinking divulged because it would have reflected unfavorably on the United Kingdom's waging of the war and that an accommodating Franklin D. Roosevelt was more than anxious to go along with him, not only because Churchill had requested it, but also because it was so important to the cementing of American-British relationships in the war.

Ironically, the sinking of the Rohna also must have helped cement the relationships between the axis powers of Germany and Japan. In fact, it was the only time in World War II when either of those two countries helped the other in actual military action. In attacking the Rohna and its convoy, Germany was helping Japan both by destroying the ship and by reducing the number of Americans who would arrive in the CBI to fight against the Nips. All twelve ships in the Mediterranean convoy were loaded with Yanks.

I have one other postscript to the sinking of the Rohna.

In August of 1945, I was on another troopship on my way home from Burma and again crossed the Mediterranean. Those of us on board asked the captain of the ship to tell us when we arrived at about the point where the Rohna was sunk. He did so and we held a memorial service for the victims.

We said some prayers and some of us wept at the memory of what happened there.

MISERY ON THE PLAINS OF INDIA

Following the attack on the Rohna, our rickety wooden ship (with steel hulls) moved on eastward as fast as it could manage. Our convoy was held up a few days at the Suez Canal to let other ships move on and into the Indian Ocean. Meanwhile, we were progressively more revolted by conditions aboard the Karoa. We had expected a ship commanded by British officers to be kept reasonably clean. But the reverse was true. Admittedly however, the laziness and life-long habits of the Indian crew caused much of the suffocating filth aboard.

We also were surprised by the brutal treatment of the Indians by their British masters. Coercion rather than education on the subjects of either cleanliness or efficiency was the British answer to every problem that arose on board. Not a day went by when I did not see one of the officers kicking or striking a crewmember. The physically small and relatively weak Indians were forced into some types of labor that would have been difficult for much larger men to perform.

The food served to us was atrocious, and the fare given to the crew was even worse. Mutton stew was served almost every day we were on the Karoa. The filth aboard was so bad that sometimes we tried to keep count of the rats scurrying into every corner of the ship. But none of it seemed to bother the British, whose officers and ship's crew could usually be found relaxing on the bridge and drinking tea or rum. I later had cause to admire and be grateful to British officers and soldiers who served so valiantly against the Japanese in the CBI Theater, particularly in their famed victory over the Nips at Imphal on the India-Burma border. But I still resented the contemptible way in which they treated the people of India.

Meanwhile, our ship churned onward while all of us aboard kept wondering what our final destination would be. The ship's officers continued to withhold that information from us. Nor could we ever tell our location. The various bodies of water all looked the same to us despite the fact that in our long voyage we had passed from the Atlantic Ocean into the Mediterranean Sea, then into the Red Sea, and along the mythical dividing line between the Indian Ocean and the Arabian Sea. But, we finally learned that we were heading into the famous Arabian Sea port of Bombay, India, Kipling's storied albeit most unattractive city.

From what we could see from the ship, we had no desire to debark and plunge into the incredible mass of people who seemed to crowd into every inch of the space available in the area near the port. Moreover, sanitary conditions appeared to be geometrically worse than they were even on the Karoa.

When Al Jolson used to shout that "You ain't seen nothin' yet", he could have been talking about what lay on the other side of Bombay from us. We learned about it two days after we arrived at the port when we finally were escorted off the ship and onto an ancient train which was to take us across the endless and desolate plains of central India to another less-than-desirable metropolis known to the world as Calcutta.

First, you must understand Indian railroads themselves, and I have heard over the years that they still have not improved to any great degree. Many of them were narrow gauged affairs, although the gauges changed throughout the country. This meant that, when a train came to the end of a stretch of narrow gauged tracks, the passengers had to transfer from one train to another, and the timing of the connections was never on the money. As a result, many thousands of American GI's spent a solid week or more traversing the Indian sub-continent over a distance relatively equal to that between New York and St. Louis.

But that was the least of the problems in 1943. While waiting in the Bombay train station, we watched Indian workmen fumigate our train and dramatically demonstrate the numerical superiority of cockroaches among the creatures on earth. I am sure we literally saw millions of the creatures scurry out of the train when the workmen attacked them with insecticides. Indeed, we wondered if the train could have moved before the fumigation because of the weight of so many of the repulsive creatures aboard it. We also learned that the seats in the trains were narrow wooden benches, which were entirely unsuitable for large American behinds.

Yet this was only the beginning of an incredibly dismal journey. While the aforementioned famine of 1943 was concentrated in the eastern part of India, its effects could be seen across the entire subcontinent. The plains of India have an extremely heavy population density and we saw living skeletons along the entire distance of our trip to Calcutta. Moreover, the people understandably seemed to resent our relative prosperity.

Due to the intense heat on the plains, all the windows on the train had to be kept open, both when the train was in motion as well as when it drew into a station. This made it easy for hundreds of starving people to pull themselves up to the relatively low windows and beg us for food. Many of them did so even when the train was in motion, yet we never saw any of them injured.

While watching these tragically deprived people was a poignant experience, to smell their body odors was repugnant. Equally as grievous and repelling were the high numbers of people who were deformed from diseases such as leprosy, elephantiasis and others. There doubtless are many CBI vets still living today who remember the beggar at one railroad station who paraded past the windows of every incoming train, carrying his huge and deformed testicles in the wheelbarrow he pushed in front of him. Nor will you find any CBI alumnus who does not recall other such victims of elephantiasis, a disease which is caused by a parasitic worm.

The plains of India were especially forbidding on our journey in 1943 because of a historic over flooding of the rice fields caused by monsoon rains of unprecedented severity. The result was such a severe shortage of India's principal source of food that it caused a huge and devastating famine. Consequently, we saw hundreds of thousands of people who were starving, as well as suffering from dread diseases. We ached with sympathy for all of them while being simultaneously re-pelled by the sight of their suffering.

Finally we arrived at that tent city near Calcutta where we experienced the incidents and conditions covered earlier in this text.

ON THE EVE OF COMBAT

When Seymour Schoenfeld and I decided to embark on the dangerous mission mentioned by the recruiting sergeant at Tent City, we all shared various kinds of speculation about the nature of it, not to mention the roles we would play as individual soldiers. But I was encouraged when the sergeant disclosed that the officers in charge of the undertaking were looking for men who had experience in mule handling. I quickly revealed that I possessed this experience, and I kept hoping that my assignment would be no more dangerous than braving Japanese fighter attacks on mule-carrying transport planes shuttling between India and Australia. But that proved to be the mother of all pipe dreams. It turned out I eventually was going to handle mules all right, but not in the manner I anticipated. Moreover, when we again boarded one of India's less-than-scrumptious trains, it was quickly evident that we were headed southwest and back into the interior of the subcontinent. Our destination turned out to be a village named Deogargh which, we learned, had a somewhat inappropriate meaning in the Hindu language. Deogargh, translated into English, meant Hand of God, and the village was anything but that.

However, the British army camp near the village was a well-organized reasonably clean affair. The army's own caste system was in effect, albeit much less rigid than the one so tightly controlled among Hindus. There were the circus-sized tents for administrative offices, large individual tents for the officers and the pup-sized affairs for enlisted men like me.

I soon learned that I was assigned to the Long-Range Penetration Group 5307 (later known as Merrill's Marauders) and that our 3,000 men were destined for combat action in the north of Burma. I also learned that the regiment-sized outfit had experienced an even tougher training program than any of those I had suffered through in the states. Yes, there were the usual long marches and tough obstacle courses, but there also was much more, including jungle tactics, mock infantry assaults, clearing and concealing jungle trails, and even practice river crossings, an endeavor which later became extremely important in the crossing of numerous and formidable streams in Burma. I was told also that there had been maneuvers of both American and British troops at Deogargh and that the Yanks beat the tar out of England's finest in mock battles.

During my own two weeks at Deogargh, I was taken on daylong hikes through the thick jungle surrounding the camp. This training was valuable, not only in learning how to move through jungle growth, but in identifying the kinds of plants, leaves and other growth we could eat safely if we ever got lost in a jungle area – a training I later was delighted to have.

Most of the men at Deogargh already had experienced the horrors of warfare and my conversations with them were far from reassuring. They were soldiers who had served in the Pacific island fighting and who agreed to volunteer for further action in Burma because they had been given the same promise Schoenfeld and I had received: that upon completion of ninety days of service in our upcoming secret mission we all would be pulled out of action and rotated back to the states. This was a highly deceitful reassurance that none of us would later forget or forgive. The GIs from the Pacific action were hardened soldiers who talked endlessly about the numbers of 'damn Japs' they had killed and who looked forward to a similar form of recreation in southeast Asia. I found this kind of braggadocio to be a bit disquieting, and I therefore tried to spend most of my time with other "greenhorns" like myself. However, I later was to treasure the survival techniques the Pacific veterans passed on to me when we went up against the Japanese in Burma. Also, many of them already had contracted malaria, dysentery and other jungle diseases before they left the islands and thus were admired for braving still more punishment in Burma.

Meanwhile, we learned that General Stilwell was getting impatient for his officers and troops to get going on a joint American-Chinese drive through north Burma, and he was irritated about the slowness of several Chinese regiments in moving into position at the jumping off place in India's Assam Province. Indeed, the mission was delayed for more than a month while Chiang Kai Shek dillydallied on approving the necessary troops essential to the campaign.

We knew we were getting very close to the start of our mission when we were told we could no longer send or receive mail to the states because of secrecy requirements. Finally, under the highly capable command of Colonel Charles Hunter, the 5307th moved out of Deogargh in another train which, if possible, was in an even more deplorable shape than the one in which we rode from Bombay to Calcutta. We started out in an uncomfortable boxcar type of conveyance, and again we stared out open windows at bleak but heavily populated landscapes. And the secrecy and danger of our assignment kept getting more apparent. We were told very little and our conversations among one another were kept to a minimum. We didn't know where we were going or what we would be doing there. We didn't know that a Quebec conference had even been held, or that it was an historic event that would decide our fate. However, the rumors were rampant, and none of them were good.

Moreover, while most of us had been taught elementary geography in school, I must acknowledge that few of us knew anything about the terrain or even the relative locations of the points in India through which we were traveling. In short, we felt like pawns that were being lifted around a complicated chessboard without any control over our movements or destinies. We also began giving more weight to our concepts of gun battles against our foes and what that unpromising activity might portend for us. It is relatively easy to volunteer for the armed forces when you are back in the states and when warfare seems likely to be little more than a football game in which you might suffer an injury or two. But the closer you get to armed confrontation with an enemy who really is going to be shooting at you, with everything from rifles to artillery and machine guns, the picture suddenly becomes a bit more threatening to one's well-being and even survival.

Soon our train arrived at one of the world's most interesting, but least known rivers. Many Americans have heard about the Yellow River in China and the Ganges River in India, but few can identify the Brahmaputra which flows two thousand miles from China in the north through a large portion of India and on south into the Bay of Bengal. It is a very wide stream at points and it is almost as holy to Indians as the Ganges. Moreover, the Ganges merges with the Brahmaputra in Bengal Province before both empty into the Bay of Bengal. As large and as long as it is, the Brahmaputra has no bridges. But it has numerous sampan boats and a few ferries. The river is host to a number of interesting creatures, including two kinds of crocodiles. One of them is the man-eating eusterine which India's natives fear more than they do tigers. The other is the gavial whose jaws are smaller than those of an eusterine and eats only fish.

After our arrival at the river, we transferred all of our weapons and equipment onto an old and dilapidated paddlewheel riverboat which was more comfortable than the train cars, and we discovered there also was a lot of interesting activity along the banks of the Brahmaputra. I shall not forget, for example, the sight of a number of skeleton-thin natives straining their muscles while, from the river's bank and with the aid of a long rope, they pulled hundred-foot flatboats upstream. All of the boats, incidentally, were loaded to the limit with various kinds of heavy cargo.

Eventually, we arrived at a point where still another train was awaiting us, this time on narrow-gauged tracks. We were again cramped for space for the two days we were on it until we reached our jumping off place for the campaign. We unloaded at the village of Ledo in Assam Province in the extreme northeast of India. Assam was famous for its English-owned tea plantations, a torrid climate in which the heat reached more than 120 degrees Fahrenheit, and the heavy monsoon rains which drenched the country. These monsoons often ranged between some three hundred to five hundred inches a year. Consequently, Assam Province was and still is known as one of the hottest and wettest locations on Planet Earth.

The village also was the site for the beginning of the new Ledo Road being constructed by American army engineers.

Most of these soldiers were black and they achieved the largest and most difficult engineering feat in American military history, carving the road for hundreds of miles through rugged mountains and some of the most menacing jungles in the world. The Ledo Road eventually extended southeast some 500 miles to connect with the storied Burma Road near Lashio. The Burma Road is famous as the passageway along the same route followed by Marco Polo on his journeys into China in the 14th Century.

Our regiment, originally given the clumsy and probably the longest designation in the American armed forces as the 5307th Composite Unit (Provisional), was now ready to begin its long march into history as the newly-recognized Merrill's Marauders, a name dreamed up at Deogargh by a newsman who wished to honor Brigadier General Frank Merrill, the commanding officer of the regiment.

Merrill himself gathered the regiment together one day on what passed for a parade ground to give us a short talk. He informed us of the decision made by Chief of Staff George Marshall in Washington to take the regiment out of the command of General Wingate and place it under the direction of General Stilwell. He also gave a brief explanation of the mission ahead for us, including the long marches we would have to make on a daily basis. But there were several things he did not tell us. He did not tell us that he had a very bad heart condition and that Stilwell was blind in one eye, almost blind in another, and, like Merrill, was in generally poor physical condition. We also learned from other sources about another omission in Merrill's talk that later caused a great deal of resentment. It concerned a deplorable decision by Merrill and General Stilwell that most of us in the Marauders did not learn about until years later.

The post-war disclosure of this decision came from Colonel Ray Peers, commander of the American O.S.S detachment which, with the assistance of Kachin tribesmen, specialized in ambushing tactics behind the Japanese lines in Burma. Peers said he had described to Merrill how the lack of Japanese air strength allowed his troops to fly unchallenged over north Burma and parachute into specified locations. General Wingate had successfully done the same thing with his Chindits whose brigade was almost as large as the Marauders' regiment. Peers therefore was dumbfounded when he learned that Merrill (obviously on the orders of Stilwell) was insisting that the Marauders march the first 200 miles of their mission over the Patkai Mountains with full packs and weapons as a "toughening" exercise. They were ordering this little assignment despite the fact that none of the enemy was in the entire area and our commanders knew this to be a fact.

Peers reported that he tried to talk Merrill out of such foolishness but was unable to do it, even though Peers and Wingate, on the basis of their prior experience, said it was much better not to exhaust troops before they actually went into combat. Therefore, Peers told Merrill, the Marauders would have much more strength and endurance when they needed it if they could omit the tough climbs over the Patkai Mountains and the Naga Hills. But Stilwell and Merrill wouldn't budge on their decision, and unfortunately they had the support of another officer who otherwise was to win the great respect of the Marauders. He was Colonel Charles N. Hunter, Merrill's second in command who, like Stilwell and Merrill, thought the extra long trek over the Patkais would toughen rather than exhaust the troops. All of these officers learned later that the incredible conditions to which we were later subjected were tough enough without any gratuitous help from the men who were deciding our fates. However, as bad as it was, the decision did not compare with the inhuman actions that Stilwell later took against the Marauders.

Most of us in the regiment also were less than impressed by the point in Merrill's talk to us when he described our forthcoming combat action as "something I know all of you have been looking forward to." I know that a number of military commanders have used the same dissembling remarks to inspire their troops, and I think it is a bit ridiculous. No soldier in his right mind looks forward to a situation in which he may be killed. At least I didn't, and I'm not afraid to admit it. And I know the same thing was true of most of my comrades. We were realistic enough to believe that our fast approaching combat action would be something we would just as soon avoid. But we never dreamed that our particular combat situation would turn out to be as loathsome as it did.

While we were still at Ledo, we also were given a short pep talk by Lord Mountbatten who had just recently been appointed the supreme commander of all troops in Southeast Asia. It was to him that Stilwell was supposed to report, although Stilwell consistently acted on his own with unilateral decisions, including the mission he was assigning the Marauders. That mission, we were told by Merrill, was one in which the Marauders, for what was promised to be a relatively short period of time, would operate behind enemy lines in north Burma. What he didn't tell us was information he did not at that time possess himself. Eventually, we would be marching and fighting all the way to the village of Myitkyina in northeast Burma, a distance which, elongated by perpetually curving trails, totaled approximately 800 miles.

We started our great adventure in the evening of February 7, 1944, Merrill deciding that our movement at night might keep the Japanese from learning about our mission. Yet, on the second night on the trail we heard a Tokyo Rose broadcast on one of our radio receivers in which that detested little lady described in some detail what we were up to. Mind you, we were marching at night with the greatest secrecy through some of the world's most remote country and the enemy was not employing any air reconnaissance in the region. Yet Tokyo Rose was telling us all about everything we were doing.

It is an understatement to say that the experience did not give us the greatest confidence in our security measures. Indeed, our own commanders had kept so much information secret from us that we wondered if the Japanese did not know more about our activity than we did. Paradoxically, the enemy did not try to attack us when we were in such vulnerable circumstances, apparently because most of the Japanese forces in north Burma were stationed a good distance south of us in the Hukawng Valley. However, the Japanese had made a mistake in not moving north to confront us before we made the difficult trek over the mountains. They could have fought from the high ground against us while we were climbing the slopes. Moreover, it was an initiative they should have taken against us if they had understood how damaging to them it would be if our forces completed the Ledo Road into the Hukawng country. At that point, we would be poised to expand the overland route all the way to China. Yet we traveled more than 300 miles from Ledo before we made contact with the Japanese near the village of Walawbum.

General Merrill nevertheless decided with good reason that we would have a tough time when we reached Walawbum against an enemy who already had been alerted to our mission and would be waiting for us in a state of readiness. But at the same time, in the light of the Tokyo Rose broadcast, he decided that night marching was not concealing our movement from the Japanese and therefore we would move forward during the daylight hours. It was a great decision as far as his soldiers were concerned. Now we not only could better detect bumps and obstacles in the road, but we could move faster and handle our weapons, our mules and our equipment much better in the daylight hours. Moreover, the process of marching at night had had its psychological drawbacks. There was something ominous and threatening about moving over mountainous territory in the dark of night toward perils yet unknown but which we knew would be terrifying.

CLIMBING A MOUNTAIN

In 1944, I was five feet, six inches tall and weighed 125 pounds. I'm sure that's why the United States army, in one of its less rational judgments, decided that on the long 800-mile march to Myitkyina I should carry on my back a 15-pound tripod and in my hands a 75-pound Browning Automatic Rifle (B.A.R.), all of which added up to a load only 35 pounds less than my body weighed. It is, therefore, no exaggeration to say that I struggled to keep up with our column when we left Ledo and headed for Shingbwiyang in northwest Burma. But I manfully plodded along, wondering each moment whether the gun would simply drop on the ground when my weary muscles could no longer keep it aloft.

We marched what our officers told us were seventeen miles the first night out of Ledo, and every mile was unadulterated torture. Not only was my gun getting heavier on each passing mile, but we were also laboring in weather in Assam that was incredibly hot and humid. I was constantly amazed at what the human body could endure, especially the one that belonged to me.

The second night's march was an estimated 20 miles in length and my exhaustion reached an undreamed-of level when we bivouacked the next morning. But I was at least partially revived when an incredible event occurred. Deep in that thoroughly isolated part of the world we were entertained by a Negro marching band, apparently culled from the black members of the Ledo Road construction crew. And the musicians played their instruments with the same skill they exhibited while operating their dump trucks and other road machinery in such challenging terrain. Whatever bigotry this Southern-born farm boy had entertained up to that moment miraculously disappeared when I was cheered by the beautiful strains of African-American music from men who were engaged with me in the challenging missions of a great war. Moreover, the experience bore fruit in later years when I became a political activist against racial prejudice in the United States. (General Louis Pick, who commanded the construction of the road, described the work of the African Americans as outstanding and at war's end issued an official commendation of their achievements.)

On the same day we heard the musicians' performance, a merciful God sent me some welcomed relief when he worked through the auspices of a large and very strong man who had been leading a mule just ahead of me in the marching column. I could never forget the kind and generous action he undertook in my behalf and I can remember his words almost verbatim to this day: "You ain't going to make it son," he said. "That load (my B.A.R. gun and tripod) is much too heavy for you, and I don't know why in hell anyone ever saddled someone your size with it. Now, no one will ever know the difference as to who is leading my mule or who is carrying your gun, so let's just trade off here."

And he not only carried through on that offer but also showed me how to pack the mule with the 81-milimeter mortar the uncomplaining beast had been carrying.

So that's how I met Jude, a courageous animal who, in effect, became my closest friend and companion on the rest of the march to Myitkyina. Acquiring him also seemed like an act of destiny, inasmuch as I had kept wanting to work with a mule, an activity in which, as mentioned earlier in this text, I had amassed a good deal of experience back home. Sadly, I never obtained the name of the generous soldier who became my benefactor and I never saw him again. The next day he apparently shifted his position closer to the head of the column, and I have reason to believe he was later killed in the combat action at Walawbum. I shall never forget him nor ever cease being grateful for the kindness which led him to such a generous action, one which surely made his own efforts on our march much more demanding. And, of course, I have been saddened through the years by the conjecture that he did not survive the march. If he did not, could it be traced to the chain of events, which began when he shouldered the tripod and the B.A.R. for me and drastically changed the nature of his own activity in the war? It is a question that will disturb me to the end of my days.

It was also on our way to Shingbwiyang that we crossed the Naga Hills where the inhabitants were the world famous headhunters. We had heard many stories about the Nagas. English owners of the huge Assam tea plantations reported to American army officers that the Nagas still came down out of the hills to try to sell human heads they had taken. They preferred opium to money for such transactions. We thought some of the stories about the Nagas were exaggerated but we learned later that a number of them were true. For instance, it was reported accurately that in the past a Naga suitor of his lady love would impress her by bringing her the head of a child because a child's head was deemed important in Naga fertility rites. And if Naga crops were going bad, it was considered important to put a head on top of a post to ward off evil spirits, an endeavor the Nagas believed would bring rain to their meager croplands.

While we didn't know how many of these stories to believe, there was no doubt that the Nagas were still taking heads when we were in their country, and probably still do, despite information to the contrary in today's encyclopedias. (See photo on page 74) Members of O.S.S. Detachment 101 had reported seeing displays of Naga heads when they went into the Naga Hills and secured the help of Nagas in the Detachment's behind-the-lines operations against the Japanese. One of the best kept secrets of the war may be that both the O.S.S. and the Marauders carried substantial quantities of opium with them to give to both the Kachins and the Nagas in return for their assistance in guiding the Americans in scouting and intelligence operations. An Arkansas friend of mine, who helped install radio communications equipment in the Naga Hills, said he used to carry large amounts of opium with him to gain the help of the Nagas in his endeavors. Money was of no value to people in this isolated part of the world, but opium was a different matter.

My only contact with the Nagas was the visit several of them made to our marching line and demonstrated the use of their crossbows. In return for this little show we gave them some American cigarettes which they seemed to think were almost as good as opium.

I did not personally see any collections of heads in the Naga country. But I later saw an impressive (if that is the word for it) display provided us by Kachin tribesmen who also had history of head hunting, and who gave us a great deal of assistance against the Japanese in Burma. But more about that later.

On our way down the Ledo Road we marched single file alongside the roadway. We stayed far enough apart that there was little or no conversation except when we stopped for breaks. We started out walking about fifty minutes and then resting for ten. However, when the going got tougher over the mountainous terrain, we hiked for only twenty-five minutes and rested for five.

Not all of our movement through the mountains was unpleasant. The moon over Burma at night was a spectacular lunar display, and the mountain temperatures were much more pleasant than the torrid days and monsoon rains we experienced in Assam.

At night we stretched out on the ground at the abandoned camps of the Ledo Road construction crews, and sleep usually came easily as a result of the expenditure of our daytime energies. We saw no sign of the enemy, but we admired the intestinal fortitude of the construction men who, in effect, were the advance troops most likely to run into the Japanese at any moment.

On about the twelfth day out on our journey, the Third Battalion, in which I was serving, turned off the road and struck out into the jungle to the east of it. This turned out to be a wide flanking or "enveloping" movement in which we were then to sweep back to the west and south to engage the Japanese at Walawbum at the head of the Hukawng Valley. In so doing we also were to flank the town of Maingkwan, which the 28th and 32nd Chinese Divisions had been trying to capture. Both Maingkwan and Walawbum were highly important to our newfound allies, the formidable Kachins, and for good reason.

The native Shans in Burma sided with the Japanese and they had persuaded the Japs to perform some hideous deeds against the Kachins in the two villages. The Shans told the Japanese how the Kachins prized their young boys, not only as their heirs and the progenitors of their race, but also as fine warriors. Therefore, the Shans told the Japanese, they should either kill or castrate all the young boys they found in the Burma towns, even those in their childhood. The Shans told the Japs that this would demoralize the Kachins and discourage their highly effective ambush attacks. Subsequently, the Japanese followed the Shans' advice. At Walabum they castrated several dozen boys and at Maingkwan they gathered a large group of them together and mowed them down with a machine gun.

But rather than discouraging the Kachins, those barbaric deeds motivated them into vicious and highly effective action against the Japanese. At first, they could use only a limited number of outdated guns they possessed and which had been given to them over the years by British officers when the weapons became obsolete. But, they later were replaced by modern weapons from their new American allies. The Kachins proved to be effective both in jungle ambushes and in pitched battles in which they fought alongside both the American O.S.S. 101 Detachment and the Marauders.

In any event, the Chinese finally captured the town of Maingkwan after we had flanked them on the way to Walawbum, and mighty was the celebration of the Kachins. The murders of their young boys in that village had been avenged.

Enter at this point the first of the three fascinating stories about the important roles a trio of young Kachin boys played in the victory of American arms in the CBI Theater, the other two being covered in the concluding chapter of this book. When we arrived at the town of Shingbwiyang we also came to the end of the completed portion of the Ledo Road. We had been alerted to the fact that trails existed which could be used in our battalion's assigned flanking mission. That, in turn, required moving through dense jungles to Walawbum. But, of course, no American in our outfit knew where the trails were, or how they should be followed through many twists and turns, sometimes through jungle so thick that a trail literally could not be seen. Luckily, a fabulous officer with the 101 O.S.S. detachment, one Pete Lutken, was then in the area and told Merrill about a Kachin hunter in the region who knew all about every trail in that part of Burma. But the hunter could not be located and, instead, his 12year-old son, Ndigu Ga, showed up to take on the assignment. According to Richard Dunlop's excellent book entitled "Behind Japanese Lines," the following conversation then occurred between Lutken and Ndigu:

"'I will go in the place of my father,' Ndigu said.

'Do you know this country?'

'Yes, I do,'

'Do you think you can get them through the jungle?'

'I went with my father." the boy replied.

A skeptical Merrill was more than a little dubious that the boy could live up to his boast, but he had no alternative to the utilization of his services. Merrill also was slightly encouraged by the fact that Kachin boys were said to reach adulthood when they were given the challenge of "quests" in the jungle; and Ndigu, at his tender age, already had completed this challenge. So the boy was given the go-ahead and accurately led the way along a hundred-mile-long trail, thereby making a significant contribution to the Marauders' war effort.

Life along this trail, however, was much more difficult than our trip on the completed portion of the Ledo Road over the Patkai Mountains. Gone were the nightly campsites, gone was a visible roadway, and gone were the pleasant temperatures. Instead, we plunged into the heat, humidity and a hostile world of insects and other threatening creatures in the Burma jungles. The most inimical of these, by far, were the omnipresent leeches. After bedding down on the ground at night, we would awake in the muggy mornings with blood dripping down our legs from the attachment of exceptionally long members of the species (nicknamed elephant leeches) who seemed progressively more difficult to dislodge. There were brown ones on the ground, red ones hanging high at the top of kunai grass, and green ones lurking about shoulder high on the branches of trees. They would chew out a triangular bit of human skin and then inject their own brand of anticoagulant to keep the hole from closing up. The constant bleeding from the pests led some of the wags in our regiment to contend that their attacks merited Purple Hearts to wounded victims. Mosquitoes also were a constant nuisance as well as a disease bearing threat. It is no hyperbole to say that few of the Marauders escaped the malarial plague on the long hike to Myitkyina, many of them so sick they were sent to a rear area hospital at Margherita in Assam.

We had traveled only a day or so down the trail when we heard about the nearby presence of General Stilwell. Subsequently, we heard that he had waded across part of the Tarung River to an island where he conferred with a few officers of the regiment. That was the only time when we saw Vinegar Joe on the entire march to Myitkyina. Never once did he officially thank the Marauders for their efforts.

Additionally, our feelings toward our commanding general were exacerbated when we learned he was offered the use of some British troops to help us in north Burma, but spurned their assistance because he didn't want "those damn limeys" to get any credit for the campaign. By so doing, Stilwell incurred the loss of more of his own countrymen than otherwise would have been required.

ASSAULT ON WALAWBUM

We soon learned that the strategy and tactics in the Burma fighting would be complicated and puzzling. First, the numbers of troops on both sides in the fighting were relatively small. Where divisions were being moved to different positions in both the European and Pacific Theatres and in the south of Burma, the war in north Burma was one in which much smaller battalions on both sides were constantly trying to outmaneuver one another. This was a situation that became extremely complicated on the Marauders' march toward Walawbum. It was one in which our enveloping movements grew out of other enveloping movements or crisscrossed them in efforts to keep the Japanese off balance and contained.

We could tell every night when we had completed a day's march that our officers' tensions were higher and that the time was drawing nearer when we would encounter the enemy. Then one night we heard sounds like thunder and learned that they were caused by Chinese artillery shelling Maingkwan.

It was perhaps three or four miles before we expected to make contact with the enemy when some of us were assigned to take a different route. Scouts reported that a patrol of Japanese was nearby and we were ordered to cut it off and scout out other areas where the enemy might be.

Shortly after we left the main trail, all kinds of firing broke out at the head of our column. It was precipitated by a sniper attack by a lone Japanese soldier who was tied high in a tree so that he wouldn't fall out or suddenly decide he didn't like what obviously was a suicide mission. He managed to wound several of our soldiers whom I saw moved back toward the main trail for medical help. But then one of our sharpshooters got the range and toppled the Jap from his perch. I later saw the sniper's body. It was riddled with bullets.

We forded four streams on our way to Walawbum. All of them included in their names the Kachin word Hka which denotes a river. We first crossed the Tanai Hka and Tarung Hka in the daytime and then forded the Tawang Hka in a scary but beautiful crossing by moonlight. Later we also forded the Nambyu Hka.

Meanwhile, platoons were being sent out on various scouting missions to determine how far east the regiment would have to swing in order to flank the Japanese. The regiment on this march regularly received supplies dropped from Dakota C-47 airplanes, also affectionately called the "Goony Birds" by all CBI personnel. In addition, the Kachin scouts capably kept us from being ambushed by the Japanese.

Then we came upon still another river. This one was destined to play an important part in the battle for Walawbum. It was named the Numpyek Hka and it flowed through the village of Walawbum. Our immediate task was to cut several roads leading to the stream and to deal with a number of Japanese patrols along the way. We could and did keep running into them at almost any point in the trails we followed, a frightening phenomenon that rarely occurred in the war action elsewhere in the world with a few exceptions on the Pacific islands. We had no fronts in the ordinary sense, and the fighting here was often (though not always) on a small group and even individual basis.

After marching south for a number of miles, the regiment turned back to the west in order to reach Walawbum and cut the Kamaing Road, a passageway which was little more than a broad and dusty trail. Eventually, the three battalions of our regiment were to swing in on Walawbum from different directions.

During all this time, Jude and I followed the riflemen in the Third Battalion, and we were given a clearly defined duty. Each time a skirmish developed a mortar crew would descend on us and help me unload the mortar from Jude's long-suffering back. Then I was directed to take Jude and myself into the always nearby jungle growth and hide there until the action was ended. But we could go only a short distance in the event I had to quickly reload Jude as the battalion moved to another location.

The closer we got to Walawbum the more intensified the action became. Eventually, the Third Battalion found itself behind one stem of a U-shaped configuration in the Numpyek River while the Japanese were behind the other stem. At that point, the Japanese decided to launch a three-day assault and the result was one of the bloodiest examples of carnage in the entire Burma campaign. As seen in the accompanying diagram on page 64, the Japanese had to cross the western stem of river, then march across the open space between the two stems, and finally try to attack the Americans who were on the other side of the eastern stem of the river.

I was on high ground on the American side when our battalion started the action by firing more than a hundred mortar shells into the concentration of Japanese across the river, a number of them from the weapon Jude had been carrying. The enemy responded with a comparable barrage, and it was then that I learned that artillery fire could be every bit as dangerous as close order combat if the gunners have got their field pieces zeroed in on your position accurately. Indeed, one can ask any soldier in any modern war to identify the most feared kinds of hostile fire and he almost always will put an artillery attack near the top of the list.

In any event we knew that our own mortar fire was effective because we could see and hear the Japanese rushing reinforcements to their men on their side of the river.

Later, the Japs tried to cross the river in one wave of soldiers after another. This culminated in close-order combat hauntingly resembling the old Cowboy-Indian battles of the American Wild West. Like the action portrayed in a good John Wayne movie we were told each time to hold our fire until the enemy was within about forty yards of us.

The Japanese attacked several times in the first two days of the action and were quite easily repulsed. But on the third day, our enemies launched an all-out assault that turned into an incredible massacre. First, the Japanese brought up more of their artillery from a rear area and began shelling us with little result, although some of it came uncomfortably close to Jude and me.

Then shouting "Susume, Susume" (meaning to move forward) and screaming their "Banzai" battle cry, the Nips splashed across their stem of the river and moved on across the open clearing before surging into our shallow stem of the stream. Many of them made it to our bank before they were cut down, and during the third day their bodies had to be stacked two or three deep at the end of each assault so that we would have room to fire when the next attack began. Even more died in the river itself. There were so many that the shoals literally turned red from the blood which was shed in them. In between attacks the Japanese and Americans traded obscene insults and the enemy would try to storm the American position again. The Nips carried 25-caliber rifles (less effective than our 30-caliber pieces) and also fired machine guns while their officers (again mirroring an American movie) waved their swords in the air and exhorted their men to greater efforts. Indeed, while I certainly held anything but kind feelings toward the Japanese during the war, I must confess my admiration for the courage they showed at Walawbum and later in the campaign. However, one had to wonder whether some of it might have been sheer masochism as the Nips seemed as intent upon their own destruction as they were on their enemy's.

In achieving that suicidal wish, the Japanese efforts were most effective. I watched for hours as the slaughter continued. It was well described by Lieutenant Ogburn in his book entitled The Marauders, as follows: "The persistence of the Japanese was horrifying. When a machine gun crew fell dead with its weapon another would rush forward, grab the heavy mechanism, carry it a few steps and then go down in their turn, only to be replaced by still another crew."

As for the Americans, a good description of their valor is contained in the diary of Major John Jones of the Third Battalion: "The spirit of the men was awe-inspiring. They didn't notice the shells whizzing by or the mortars exploding in their perimeter. Some of them stood up and shook their fists, imploring the Japs to come on."

Eventually, the Nips had to abandon their efforts and American officers later counted more than 400 dead Japanese in and around the river. The American fatalities? Incredibly there were none, and only seven Marauders were wounded. However, we were nearly out of ammunition when the Japs decided to end their attacks. Did the Japanese make this decision because they, too, were running low on ammunition? No one will ever know, but I suspect that this was the case and the reason why we finally were able to prevail over a stubborn enemy.

In other action the First and Second Battalions in and around Walawbum killed an estimated 500 Japanese in scattered skirmishes. This brought the number to 800 or more enemy dead at Walawbum, incredibly compared with only eight fatalities on the American side. However, jungle diseases proved to be much more costly to the Marauders than enemy gunfire. Since the regiment had started its march in Assam some 300 or more of our soldiers had been put out of action by malaria, dysentery and other similar maladies, with all of the victims sent back to the rear area hospital at Margherita in Assam. Yet this was almost insignificant compared with the number who fell victim to diseases by the end of the campaign in Burma. In that respect, the American experience in Southeast Asia was reminiscent of the soldiers of the blue and the gray in the American civil war when, as in our case, the germs killed or disabled more soldiers than did the bullets.

When the firing had completely stopped at Walawbum the mortar crews were waiting on us "muleskinners" to pack the mortars back on our animals and prepare for the next move of the regiment. As a reward for the success of our first mission we were blessed with an airdrop of K-rations for us and other kinds of food for our animals. The rice the Japanese had left behind in their hurry to escape from the Walawbum area further alleviated our hunger. Moreover, our morale increased significantly when we were told that our spearheading efforts enabled the Chinese in the rear of us to advance more in five days than they previously had moved forward in five months.

It was midnight after the third day of combat when our regiment, after cleaning up operations, pulled out of the Walawbum area and marched a few miles north to the village of Wesu Ga. Then, on the next day, we headed east toward the relatively pleasant village of Shikau Ga. There, for two whole days, we enjoyed ourselves, swimming in still another river while some of us cavorted naked on the sands of its beach. The mules enjoyed themselves, too, and Jude splashed around in the water to his equestrian content, if equestrian is an adjective which may be applied to mules as well as to horses. In point of fact, I would have preferred Jude to a horse any day of the week on our long journey toward Myitkyina. Every moment I felt closer to that courageous animal who was still to share with me more hardships and dangers. He also won recognition for being a larger and calmer beast of burden than most of the others in our battalion.

At Shikau Ga we received more air drops of food, supplies and ammunition from our ever faithful C-47 Goony Birds. Their pilots already were flying tons of supplies and weapons over the Himalayan Hump to Kunming, a Western China metropolis which still had been kept out of the hands of the Japanese.

I was among those who were ordered to recover the Shikau Ga supplies after they hit the ground. This was not a task to be taken lightly. Some of the food for our mules was dropped without the help of a parachute, and the hard containers carrying it always hit the ground like bombs. Once in a while they struck soldiers or mules and seriously injured or even killed them.

Our morale, after completion of our first mission, was relatively high. But the secrecy which had plagued us ever since the formation of the Marauders regiment remained the Standard Operating Procedure of its officers. Not once after leaving Deogargh had we been told the location or number of our target towns, how far we would have to walk and fight against the enemy, how frequently we could expect major battles, and how many of them were to be anticipated. The only thing we were told (as mentioned earlier in this text) was that our mission would last only ninety days and that we then would be rotated back to the states. This was a reward for volunteering for a dangerous assignment that was never described to us.

Consequently, we thought that Walawbum was the only battle in which we would have to fight, inasmuch as we had left the training camp in Deogargh in late January and it already was nearly the middle of March when we chased the Japs out of the area. So, we thought, we had triumphed at Walawbum quicker than was expected and it was the only engagement in which we would have to participate. This, of course, came under the assumption that the several hundred thousand British, Indian and Chinese troops in Burma would be able to handle the rest of the liberation of the northern part of the country. In fact, we had been told we were to spearhead the Chinese only temporarily, and that once we had given them the momentum they needed they would be able to conquer the rest of north Burma, particularly since reports persisted that Stilwell had persuaded Chiang Kai Shek to send some entire divisions to Burma to finish the job of driving the Japanese out of the country. (He finally provided only a very small fraction of the more than 36 divisions he had at his disposal.)

In view of all this, the fact that the successful action at Walawbum required only a few days was just an amazing bit of luck and we thought we would soon be homeward bound after the Chinese divisions arrived.

But we should have learned by that time that the continued blanket of secrecy under which our officers never gave us any information would again turn out to mean bad news was headed our way.

Blood in the Hukwang Valley

We were shocked and angered when we awoke one morning at Shikau Ga and received orders to load the mules and prepare to move out for another combat mission. The next destination, we were told, would be south of us in the area of a village named Shaduzup.

Moreover, our many miles of more marching and more fighting in order to get there culminated with the most bloody mission ever fought by the Marauders and their allies, the Kachins and the Chinese, although, once again, the Chinese brought up the rear with the Marauders spearheading the offensive.

The primary objective of our new mission was to take control of the highly strategic Hukawng Valley. In so doing, we found our movement to the south to be tough going. The jungles were thick with heavy underbrush and high elephant grass. We had to use machetes in order to get any forward motion for our pack animals and ourselves. The humid heat and the hordes of insects that followed and attacked us wherever we went exacerbated the roughness of the terrain. Malaria, dysentery, dengue fever and utter fatigue were exhausting our endurance and diminishing our mental and physical will to carry on, to keep putting one foot in front of another with the constant awareness that the enemy might be found around the next turn in the trail. In fact, our struggle against the hostile environment, in addition to the amount and ferocity of the warfare we knew we were going to face, required a reservoir of courage and endurance in each of us that I am sure most of us never dreamed was so deep. The impact on all of us was eloquently described in Charlton Ogburn's book as follows: "The physical exhaustion resulting from seven weeks of marching through mountains and jungles and mud and water, from insufficient food, and from disease, probably made us more susceptible to the nervous strain of always being in the enemy's territory. This was the worst part of our experience. Not to know from one instance to the next, week after week, when the silence would explode around you it created a suspense difficult to describe. Every time a twig crunched under your foot it jarred your nerves because of the way it echoed inside your helmet; the echo always made it sound as if it came from (the jungle) off to the side from where an ambush would be."

The strategy employed in the maneuvering for the battle at Walabum was employed again for the march to the Shaduzup area at the other end of the valley. And again it proved to be successful, although with even greater blood-shed than the torrent at the confrontation along the Numpyek River. Basically, this approach followed a pattern of dispatching part of the regiment in broad encircling movements in which we would cut the Kamaing Road to the south and in the rear of the Japanese troops at Shaduzup. Simultaneously, part of the regiment would surprise the enemy with another enveloping movement to cut the road to the north and in front of the Japanese forces.

But in the Hukawng Valley the strategy involved some more complicated maneuvering than it did at Walawbum. The First Battalion was sent out a day or two ahead of the other two with the mission of cutting the road above and below Shaduzup, some 30 miles below Walawbum as the crow flew, but more than twice that distance along the in-and-out-of-the-jungle route taken by the battalion to avoid detection by the enemy. The 113th Chinese regiment provided back-up strength. Meanwhile, the Second and Third Battalions followed up with longer and more circuitous routes farther east from the Kumaing Road. Their mission was to swing in on the road at the tongue-twisting village of Inkangatawng about ten or fifteen miles south of Shaduzup.

Again, our Kachin allies proved to be invaluable. They knew of trails that had never been discovered by the Japs in the wilderness of thick brush, high elephant grass and copses of bamboo. The latter was of more than passing interest to Jude because he and the other mules treated bamboo shoots like delicacies.

One of the first assignments of my Third Battalion Company on our march to the Shaduzup region was to attack an unknown number of Japanese in an area where they were still receiving supplies along the Kamaing Road. We were to cut the road to stop the Japanese traffic on it while an air corps squadron was assigned the jobs of bombing some bridges and supporting us with strafing missions.

The Japanese appeared to be everywhere when we came to the designated area to cut the road. We were moving through elephant grass so tall it was over our heads when the enemy first came into view only about 20 yards away from us. We surprised them so effectively that at first they acted like crazed animals, running in every direction. But they soon regrouped and we spent the entire day repelling a total of at least fifteen attacks they made against us. The Japanese seemed to be everywhere in the area, and they launched charges against our lines from all four directions. In the first two of these assaults, we mowed so many of them down with machine guns and carbines that some of them in the second wave fell on top of the bodies of their own soldiers.

The mortar Jude was carrying was quickly taken off his back and put into effective use. As always, my orders were to dig a foxhole and protect myself until the orders came to move the mortar to another location. I followed orders but it bothered me to be relatively safe from enemy gunfire while Jude remained unprotected out on the open ground.

Near sundown, the Japs finally gave up and melted away into the jungle. But, throughout the rest of the way, we kept running into Japanese patrols and engaged in firefights with them.

At the same time, we also experienced some interesting and/or enjoyable incidents before we arrived at our destination.

The first of these was interesting but not enjoyable. Since we went in and out of the Chindwin Hills country we kept running into Kachin villages where we learned that our friendly little allies were not always so friendly to those they considered their enemies, including both Shans and other Kachins. There was a long history of head hunting in these villages and it was a weird experience for us to march through them and see shrunken heads fastened to posts outside the basha homes.

But the Kachins were always cheerful and friendly in their dealings with us. They seemed to want us to be happy and did their best to entertain us. As one example, they discerned that we Americans might get a kick out of riding elephants we saw along the way. Most of these remarkable animals exhibited exceptional skill and intelligence in work at Kachin-operated teakwood sawmills in the valley. I became one of the lucky riders on an elephant, but Jude was kept a long way off. Mules and elephants simply did not get along well and it was best to keep them at a distance from one another.

We deeply sympathized with the Kachins because of the treatment they had received from the Japanese invaders of their country. Japanese atrocities against the Kachins were particularly abhorrent in and along the Hukawng Valley. In fact, Japanese officers now were ordering the torturing and killing of entire Kachin families instead of restricting their activity to the victimizing of small boys. The O.S.S.101 Detachment reported that the Japanese were shooting men, women and children and, on other occasions, were slicing them up with sabers. Even more despicably they submitted many Kachin victims to the "water treatment". O.S.S. Commander Ray Peers and several members of his unit reported that the Japanese were "brutal and sadistic" in the way they perpetrated torture. Peers, his testimony supported by members of his intelligence unit, said that "The victims were tied and spread on the ground and water was continually dripped into their mouths until their systems could no longer handle it. Then repeated thumps or jumps on the abdomen caused untold pain."

On the other hand, Author Richard Dunlop, who also was a member of the O.S.S. Detachment, told of the more imaginative and agonizing procedure devised by some Kachins in taking revenge on their Japanese tormentors. He reported that Kachin captors of Japanese prisoners occasionally jammed thin slivers of bamboo up their victims' penises and then set fire to them.

After the Marauders' long march south the First Battalion surprised the enemy in the Shaduzup area and, with the aid of the Chinese regiment, held off strong Japanese counter attacks. But things became much more difficult for all three battalions when we reached our objectives in an area bounded by four villages with strange sounding names. The first three were Hsamsingyang, Nhpum Ga and Auche from where a detachment of my Third Battalion swung west to Inkangatawng on the Kamaing Road.

Upon reaching this region we learned that the Japanese forces in the area were much larger than we anticipated, and we made almost immediate contact with them. Many of them were coming up from the south and had moved around the roadblock which our advance forces from the First Battalion had set up between Kamaing and Inkangatawng.

In my battalion the action began one morning when we could hear the rumble of enemy trucks coming up one of the few and dusty roads in the area. They stopped before they reached our immediate vicinity and our officers told us we would launch a surprise attack on the Japanese convoy early the next morning. This was news that didn't faze our seasoned veterans from the South Pacific, but I will be honest enough to say it scared the hell out of me. However, all five feet, six inches and 125 pounds of me struggled manfully to present a courageous demeanor to my comrades.

Thankfully, our raid was highly successful and the Japanese were startled out of their wits when we showed up in the early morning at their bivouac area. We launched an attack with every bit of firepower we had and with every kind of weapons we were carrying. Then we pulled out as suddenly as we had appeared, after killing or wounding a goodly number of the enemy.

But we were not done for the day. A few hours later we showed up at a river where a squadron of our formidable P-51 fighter planes had blown a bridge. We found a sizeable number of Japanese wading across the stream and again we surprised them and virtually destroyed the entire unit.

Later, we lay all night on our side of the Inkangatawng River and fired mortars and other weapons to protect some of the First Battalion troops on the other side who were moving into a better tactical position. We were alarmed when we heard trucks and troops moving continuously through the night with supplies and equipment to reinforce Japanese troops north of where we were dug in and holding our positions. At daylight the Japanese attacked in force and it looked like we were in for a lot of trouble. We fired back at them with machine guns, mortars, and all the small arms and grenades we had available. Later in the morning there was a lull in the battle until the enemy regrouped and started attacking again with more determination than before. Things looked bleak for our prospects until suddenly we heard the drone of approaching small aircraft. You can't possibly realize the full extent of our exhilaration when the fighter planes turned out to be our fast and highly maneuverable P51s. And did they ever do a job! For an hour or more they strafed Jap troops and unleashed bombs on them and their equipment.

The aerial attack was highly successful to the extent that it slowed Japanese artillery and small arms fire long enough for us to regroup and replenish our ammunition.

But the Japs were far from done. Moreover, our morale was dangerously low from exhaustion and the lack of food and water for two days and nights. Even our mules were catching shrapnel and small arms fire, and a number of them went down for the count. However, Jude not only survived but he continued to maintain a relatively calm demeanor.

The battle lasted for several days until the Japanese attacks slowed down and the enemy troops began moving out to the south. We had managed to win another major engagement (in addition to all our jungle skirmishes) but the worst was yet to come. We were moving into a bloody confrontation that was The Battle of Nhpum Ga, pronounced as Na-poom Gaw. Unfortunately, it will never receive the recognition it deserves, even though it should be accorded the kind of importance attached to such American military achievements as those at Guadacanal and Iwo Jima in the Pacific. Nhpum Ga was and is the most forgotten major battle in the most ignored theater of operations in World War II. It lasted for twelve long, bloody and terrifying days, and the issue remained in doubt until the last moments of it.

PHOTO GALLERY

HMS Rhona

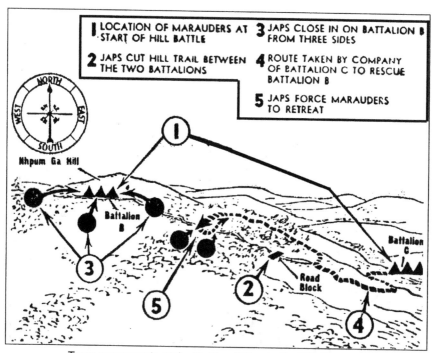

Troop movements at the Battle of Nhpum Ga Hill, First Part

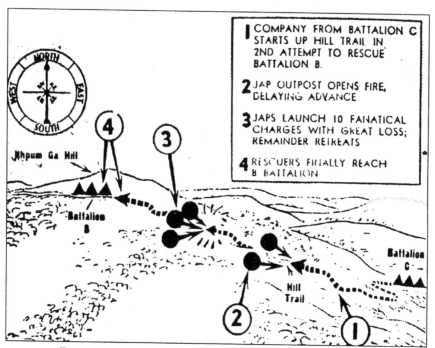

Troop movements at the Battle of Nhpum Ga Hill, Second Part

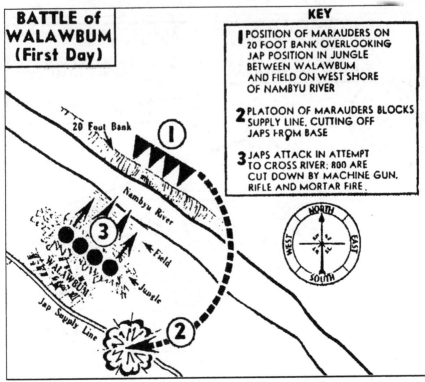

BATTLE of WALAWBUM (First Day)

KEY

1. POSITION OF MARAUDERS ON 20 FOOT BANK OVERLOOKING JAP POSITION IN JUNGLE BETWEEN WALAWBUM AND FIELD ON WEST SHORE OF NAMBYU RIVER

2. PLATOON OF MARAUDERS BLOCKS SUPPLY LINE, CUTTING OFF JAPS FROM BASE

3. JAPS ATTACK IN ATTEMPT TO CROSS RIVER; 800 ARE CUT DOWN BY MACHINE GUN, RIFLE AND MORTAR FIRE.

20 Foot Bank

Nambyu River

Field

WALAWBUM

Jungle

Jap Supply Line

Troop movements at the Battle of Walawbum, Day one

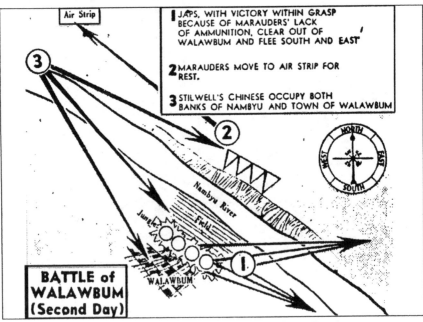

Air Strip

1. JAPS, WITH VICTORY WITHIN GRASP BECAUSE OF MARAUDERS' LACK OF AMMUNITION, CLEAR OUT OF WALAWBUM AND FLEE SOUTH AND EAST

2. MARAUDERS MOVE TO AIR STRIP FOR REST.

3. STILWELL'S CHINESE OCCUPY BOTH BANKS OF NAMBYU AND TOWN OF WALAWBUM

Nambyu River

Jungle

Field

BATTLE of WALAWBUM (Second Day)

WALAWBUM

Troop movements at the Battle of Walawbum, Day two

American and Chinese troops marching down the Ledo Road being constructed by American Engineers. February, 1944

Mule carrying 81mm mortar ammunition and muleskinner on Ledo Road.

Marauders and a pack mule passing through a village on the way to Myitkyina

Author with two Chinese soldiers at Bhamo, Burma

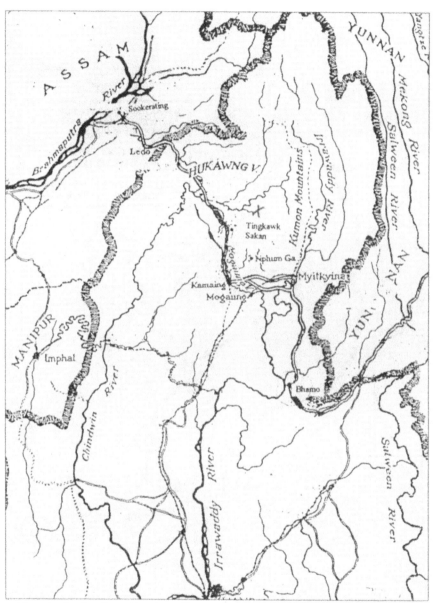

X marks the landing strip where Fred met Jack Starkey, pilot of a P51 mustang.

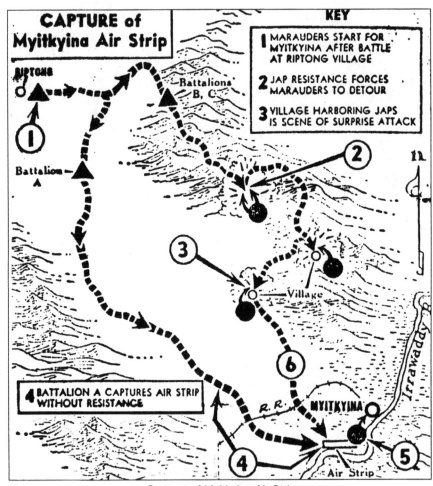

Capture of Myitkyina Air Strip

Seymour Shoenfeld and Fred Randle in Calcutta, India waiting for transport home

1St Battalion of the 475th Infantry Headquarters in the Jungle near Bhamo, Burma
Author pictured in lower left

Piles of empty 75 mm Howitzer shells after firing against the enemy

Generals Merrill and Stillwell in Burma

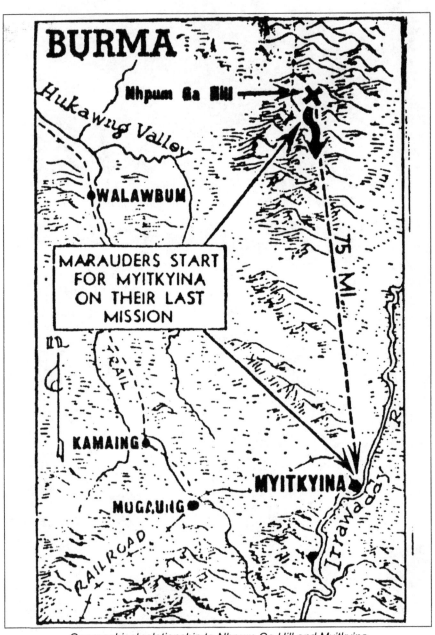

Geographical relationship to Nhpum Ga Hill and Myitkyina

Supplies airdropped into a clearing in the Burma jungle.

Naga Head hunters with young victims

HEADQUARTERS
FIRST BATTALION 475TH INFANTRY
CHINESE COMBAT COMMAND (PROV)
UNITED STATES FORCES
CHINA THEATRE

APO 627
28 May 1945

Major Gen. Frank D. Merrill
USF IB, Headquarters,
APO 885

Dear General Merrill,

In reference to your letter (To All Members of 5307th Composite Unit (Prov), dtd 7 June 1944, we take this opportunity in writing you direct.

We are three officers and eighteen enlisted men who participated in training and all combat activities of the 5307th Composite Unit from 15 January 1944 up to the inactivation of the regiment. Since that time we have all served with the 475 Infantry in action through the Centeral Burma Camp-aign.

Due to the fact we left the States 4 October 1943 instead of the month of September, we were classified ineligible to be returned to the United States with the rest of the "Marauders", the first part of April who had only fourteen more days over seas than us. Now we are stuck in the China Theatre with not nearly enough points to be returned to the States and no rotation or temporary duty to look forward too.

Using my situation as an example and the others are similar, you can see the reason we are low on points and still feel we are'nt being given a fair deal. I have been in the army twenty-five months and served twenty overseas. During this time overseas I spent a month in North Africa, and endured several enemy bombings in the Mediterranean Sea, participated in both Burma campaigns and am now enduring the most monotonous part I have been through yet.

We are sure you will understand the unfairness we feel we have been dealt and would appreciate very much any assistance you could give for our return to the states as the rest of the "Marauders" were. We have no one here to ask for help or give us any backing.

The names of these officers and enlisted men can be submitted at your request with any other information you desire.

Many thanks for any help you can give and all the trouble it has caused.

(For 3 Officers and 18 Enlisted Men:)

Fred E. Randle Jr. (37611647)
Sgt., 1st Bn., 475th Infantry

HEADQUARTERS
UNITED STATES FORCES
INDIA BURMA THEATER

A.P.O. 885
31 May 1945

Sgt Fred E. Randle Jr. 37611647
Hq. 1st Bn. 475 Infantry,
A.P.O. 627, Local.

Dear Randle:

You have asked me a fair question and I will give you a square answer with no baloney added to explain why I can't help you.

The remaining men from the Marauders were not sent back as a group. They just happened to be the largest group of men who could qualify under a special quota premitted by the War Department. This special quota came about this way. There were a certain number of combat replacements available in excess of requirements. This excess could have been sent off to another theater for use. However in preference to this, we asked and secured permission to use these replacements so that an equal number of men with long combat service could go home earlier. All of us wished we could have sent all of you back but this was impossible. The men with combat service with the Chinese regiments had to given equal consideration since some had been out here and in combat much longer than you.

A study to fill a certain quota say for combat people may look something like this:

Months Overseas	Infantry	Chinese Liaison	Cumulative Total
34	0	28	28
33.5	1	22	51
33.0	22	18	91
---	---	---	---
---	---	---	---
18.0	182	55	1981
17.5	200	200	2381

Now say you have authority to return 1980 men. Instructions can then be issued to the two units to send all men with 18 or more months services to a Replacement Depot for transportation home. Then you will see that the difference between 1981 and 2381 men or 400 men will have only 15 days less overseas service and while it may be tough on them, there is nothing that can be done about it. This is exactly the way your case worked out. While it is hard to take, there is only one way to look at it – that since all couldn't go, some had to be unlucky in order that others could get home.

Actually the April crowd that went caused considerable resentment amongst the service troops who while admitting that combat men should get some preferential treatment, felt that almost a years difference in overseas service was too much and looked like we were giving too many breaks to the combat troops. However in the April bunch we were restricted to selecting men from combat units.

Rotation is over it is true but readjustment took its place. Temporary duty has been suspended only because there is no transportation available. For the last six months every boat space and every plane seat has been taken and we couldn't send another man if we wanted to.

Figuring on these things is a damn sight worse that fighting the Japs and regardless of how hard you try to be fair you are an S.O.B. to someone.

I'm really sorry I can't help you and have given you an honest answer. Whatever you think about me on this deal, at least give me credit for not handing you a line of bull about "There is still a big war out here to fight". Please show this to all the other interested because I will go nuts if I have to answer another letter giving so much detail.

Hope you all are reasonably happy aside from having gripes about not going home. Keep you shirts on and your noses clean and sometime you will be lucky. As closely as I can figure, there are about 300 of the original gang left scattered all over the two theaters and you can rest assured that if I ever see a way clear to get you a break you will get it although up where you are anything we propose here is subject to concurrence of the Chinese Theater.

Very Sincerely,

FRANK D. MERRILL,
Major General,
Deputy Theater Commander.

77

APO 627
16 June 1945

SPECIAL ODRERS:

NUMBER.....166:   E-X-T-R-A-C-T
*   *   *   *   *

37.   Par 7 SO 154 this Hq dtd 4 June 1945 is hereby revoked.

38.   The VOCG of 30 May 1945 that:
"The following named O are reld fr asgmt to and dy with this Hq are asgd to Hq USF CT APO 879 are pl on DS with Hq SOS CT APO 627 and will rpt to CG thereof for dy with Courier Transfer Officer:

2D LT	RAYMOND E BRUNS	01 052 690 Inf SSN 1452
2D LT	MAURECE D FRASH	01 325 746 Inf SSN 4514
2D LT	EDWARD R LEE	01 062 513 Inf SSN 1452

EDCMR 4 June 1945.
No T involved. PCS.:

is hereby confirmed and made of record.

39.   PAC in Radio CRAX 7857 HQ USF IBT APO 885, WD Radio 58709 and WD Cir 8, 1945 the following named O and EM are reld fr asgmt to 475th Inf Regt CCC APO 627 are atchd unasgd to Repl Depot No 2 SOS APO 496 and WP via first available T fr APO 627 to APO 496 rptg upon arrival to CO thereof for first available air of water T to the U. S. They will rpt to Reception Station APO 627 prior to proceeding to APO 496:

1ST LT	LWEIS D BURT	01 318 411 Inf SSN 1542-7
1ST LT	STANLEY DUMSHA	01 318 525 Inf SSN 1542-7
1ST LT	EDWIN A ROTHCHILD	01 303 548 Inf SSN 2110-5
1st Sgt	Henry E Hoot	6 959 216 Inf SSN 653
T Sgt	Leo N Przeborowski	36 347 482 Inf SSN 653
T Sgt	James H Saunders	33 577 567 Inf SSN 405
T Sgt	John D Nells	14 130 545 Inf SSN 766
T Sgt	George D Alton	33 671 944 Inf SSN 651
T Sgt	Arthur F Lichte	37 308 358 Inf SSN 821
T Sgt	James T Nasengil	34 505 385 Inf SSN 766
T Sgt	Frank L Mulholland	36 511 942 Inf SSN 776
T Sgt	Bernard C Speth	33 680 601 Inf SSN 806
Sgt	Floyd B Branthafer	33 756 842 Inf SSN 653
Sgt	Donald S Chambers	36 452 959 Inf SSN 653
Sgt	Fred E Randall Jr	37 611 647 Inf SSN 405
Sgt	Seymour Schoenfeld	32 887 471 Inf SSN 653
Sgt	John B Slowey	33 319 696 Inf SSN 174
Tec 4	Elmer G Bennet	13 107 429 Inf SSN 776

R-E-S-T-R-I-C-T-E-D   (CONTD)

(SO 166 RE HQ USF CT APO 627, 16 June 25 Contd)

Tec 4	Alfred F Calfapietra	32 899 359 Inf SSN 741
Tec 4	Earl D Crain	36 486 142 Inf SSN 806
Tec 4	Howard E Elick	36 855 332 Inf SSN 056
Tec 4	Kenneth J Kilpatrick	34 804 045 Inf SSN 044
Tec 4	Maurice P T Pyne	35 230 664 Inf SSN 745
Tec 4	Pete F Spanelli	20 323 580 Inf SSN 094
Tec 4	Charles R Wehrle	35 216 006 Inf SSN 766
Cpl	Jack W Post	16 076 133 Inf SSN 653
Tec 5	Floyd D Dickerson	37 521 987 Inf SSN 531
Tec 5	Johnnie E Johnson	34 765 518 Inf SSN 607
Tec 5	William E Nugent	18 046 548 Inf SSN 712
Tec 5	Earl J Remal	31 262 245 Inf SSN 776
Tec 5	Francis J Trappen	6 851 423 Inf SSN 745
Tec 5	William J Nagy	36 730 204 Inf SSN 776
Pfc	Victor J DeLello	32 866 922 Inf SSN 745
Pfc	Richard W Dicks	35 099 713 Inf SSN 521
Pfc	Joseph N Fishel	36 421 638 Inf SSN 776
Pfc	Allie W Kleingardener	32 878 717 Inf SSN 745
Pvt	Billy B Bottis	34 774 728 Inf SSN 607
Pvt	Allen D Hines	37 522 449 Inf SSN 607
Pvt	Elwood J Hormewell	32 713 078 Inf SSN 060
Pvt	Frederick W Fasater	37 077 155 Inf SSN 094
Pvt	Neuman S Lundy	37 555 206 Inf SSN 604
Pvt	Frank J Sullivan	31 267 508 Inf SSN 745

EDCMR 30 June 1945

Travel by air rail and/or any other available means of T is auth.
Priority for this travel is APR - 4 - KNG - 12130 - AGF - GRP 42.

They will notify their correspondents and publishers to discontinue mailing letters and publications to them until further advised of their new mailing address. WDAGO Form 971-1 dtd 9 Oct 43 (V-Mail Notice to Correspondents and Publishers) may be used for this purpose.

Travel alws: WD Cir 356, 1945 VR 35-4520.
TDF. FC3. 78-207 T 431-02-03 212/50425.

*   *   *   *   *

BY COMMAND OF LIEUTENANT GENERAL WEDEMEYER:

> D. L. WEART
> Major General, USA
> Deputy Chief of Staff

OFFICIAL:

GERALD L MOLLOY
Captain, A. G. D.
Asst. Adjutant General

THE BATTLE OF NHPUM GA

After the fighting in the Inkangatawng area, our battalion was ordered to move out toward the hills to the east of us. The Third had been split up into several groups to meet the Japanese assaults and our first task was to regroup until the battalion was a coordinated unit again.

On our way toward this reconsolidating we came to a clearing that was created to accommodate an airstrip. Cut from the extremely dense jungle in the area it had become a home to our cherished P51s. On the way there, we had the chance to listen in to the pilots' radioed instructions to one another on the locations to attack, giving identification code names that emphasized different colors — such as Dragonfly Blue, Dragonfly Green, etc.

We had no sooner reached the strip, and were taking a rest break, when I learned what a small world we were fighting in. I saw a pilot walking by who looked familiar to me. I didn't say anything at first because I had forgotten his name. But it came to me just as he returned to our area and I called out to him "Aren't you Jack Starkey from Mountain View, Missouri?" He looked blankly at me for a moment and then replied: "Yes, I am, who are you?" I told him I was Fred Randle from that same small town, and he was truly astonished. We visited a while and I learned that he had experienced more than his share of excitement as the pilot who was flying a Dragonfly Blue Mustang in his squadron.

Starkey also became the second "angel" in my experience in the Burma war. The first was the unidentified soldier who gave me Jude and the mortar to load on his back in a swap for the heavy BAR machine gun I had been carrying on my person. Starkey, in turn, noticed that my shoes were completely worn out from the several hundred miles of marching I had endured after we left Assam. He told me to stay right where I was while he went on an unidentified scouting mission. About ten minutes later, he returned with a brand new pair of paratrooper boots which miraculously fit me perfectly. I sometimes wonder if I ever could have survived without them in the arduous weeks still ahead of us.

We didn't stay at that airstrip long. Our Kachin scouts informed us that Japanese forces were pressing on us from the south and west and that we needed to move fast to stay ahead of them. We received information that the Japanese had some artillery (something we did not possess) and that some of these large and heavy weapons were loaded on backs of elephants.

By this time, we had marched 70 miles from Wallabum in five days, fought at least ten skirmishes and one major battle. We also had made innumerable river crossings in the anything but monotonous terrain in the jungles of Burma.

When the Second and Third Battalions reached Nhpum Ga, the Second was ordered to hold that hilltop village against a large Japanese force coming up from the south. Meanwhile, we in the Third were ordered to proceed another four miles north to the village of Hsamshingyang where we were to build a dirt airstrip for small liaison planes needed in that area. Unfortunately, the Japanese succeeded in cutting the only trail between the two villages, thus isolating the Second Battalion and keeping the Third bottled up at Hsamshingyang.

Thus began the siege of Nhpum Ga, in which the Japanese surrounded and isolated our Second Battalion on a hill with a North-South perimeter which extended for only about 300 yards and an east-west perimeter which was even shorter. Meanwhile, the enemy not only kept the trail to Hsamshingyang blocked, but also deployed a large number of troops in the jungles around it. Thus they were in position to strongly ambush any of our attempts to open such an important trail. The upshot of the situation was that the Japanese kept failing in their attempt to capture Nhpum Ga Hill, but they were successful in keeping the Third Battalion from coming to the assistance of the Second. Unfortunately, the First Battalion was still locked in battle with the Japanese in the Shaduzup area some 40 miles away and could not yet be of any assistance in the Nhpum Ga action.

Darkness fell on the last day of the march before we could reach Hsamshingyang, but we arrived at the village just before daylight the next morning. Soon after daybreak I received orders on where to place the 81mm mortar Jude was carrying. I then was assigned the duty of helping other men pick up air drops of food and ammunition and carrying them to the front lines of our troops, four miles away at Nhpum Ga. This meant that Jude and I had to take a lot of evasive action to avoid Japanese in the jungle terrain we had to cross. To meet this challenge we once again had the stellar assistance of the Kachins and their amazing scouting ability. Time after time, they warned us when Japanese patrols were close by.

Whenever we picked up a drop we would hear the drone of C47 cargo planes coming in from a distance and soaring directly over our position. They dropped most of our supplies by parachutes, which we gave to the Kachins. They, in turn, used the silk in them for clothing and other everyday uses they had for it. Chutes were not used for the grain dropped for our mules. Instead, it was dropped in bags that occasionally burst when they hit the ground. This made no difference to Jude, the big mule eating anything and everything he found and wherever he discovered it. Let me say that we soldiers welcomed the K-rations dropped from the planes just as enthusiastically. It is my considered estimate that we had been without food on at least a fourth of the days we had spent on the trail all the way from India. Moreover, the toll continued to mount from jungle diseases, especially malaria, dysentery, and dengue fever.

After a few days had elapsed in the battle of Nhpum Ga, our officers in the Third Battalion wisely decided that the Marauders needed more firepower if we were to make any headway in lifting the siege. Specifically, we required larger and heavier guns if we were to compete with the artillery being thrown at us.

Two 75 mm Howitzers, it was decided, would be just the ticket. And, Jude and I were assigned an important role in getting one of those big guns into action. I learned about it when word came down that the two artillery pieces would be parachuted in sections by our now famous "Goony Birds", the highly reliable C-47 transports. At the same time the responsibility for assembling and operating the Howitzers would be given to a colorful sergeant by the name of John 'Red" Acker who, in fact, had been the one to suggest the project in the first place. If the Japanese could move artillery into the area by elephants, we certainly could by airplane, Red allowed. In fact, Red was quite a guy. A sergeant in the tough New Guinea campaign he was one of the veterans of the Pacific islands action who volunteered their valuable services with the Marauders. He had been an artilleryman in New Guinea, and he kept urging the use of How-itzers by the Marauders. Finally, he found a willing ear in the person of a Major Ed Briggs. Briggs, in turn, relayed the idea to Merrill and to Colonel Charles Hunter, the man who succeeded Merrill as commander of the regiment when Merrill suffered a heart attack in the Nhpum Ga action.

Acker also knew some men who could operate the big guns once they were assembled. So the officers gave the go-ahead to the project in which Jude and I were proudly to become key players. (I knew Jude liked the idea because I asked him in my best Muletese.)

Acker had quietly inspected the various mules and their handlers and eventually he came to me and asked if I would like to help in transporting the two guns that were to be dropped by parachute into a nearby clearing. They would be dropped in parts and we then would transport these parts to the front lines on the northern outskirts of Nhpum Ga Hill where the guns would be assembled. I quickly answered with a joint response for both Jude and me, inasmuch as my beloved animal still couldn't bray affirmatively as a result of the removal of his voice box.

That is how I became one of the essential participants in a project that probably had no precedent in the history of human warfare.

All went as planned.

Twelve men and their mules were selected for the endeavor and we all made an impressive parade as we left our bivouac area for the designated clearing for the airdrops. The weather conditions for the drops were perfect (no monsoon storms) and we were reasonably sure the clearing area was free of enemy soldiers. Most of the Japanese, we knew, were at that time maintaining a defensive position on a plateau near Nhpum Ga where our battalion's Orange Combat Team was engaging the enemy. The attack had only limited success and our casualties included a number of killed and seriously wounded in the effort. But the attack kept the enemy's attention focused elsewhere while we carried out the artillery drop project.

Our mules were kept close together when we took them to the area for the pick-up. Soon after we arrived we could tell by the sound of their engines when the C-47 transport planes were approaching the clearing that, fortunately, was completely free of trees and other jungle growth. It was an exciting view when we saw the first parachutes open and sail down to the earth with a section of one of the guns. Two chutes were required for each part of the guns that was dropped, one chute vertically above the other and attached to it. Subsequently, all the others descended and landed in perfect condition. Each of the two guns was parachuted in six pieces with one piece in each two-chute drop, and we all moved quickly to recover each piece.

Acker immediately demonstrated that he knew how to assemble all the sections and put the guns in firing order. But in order to fire them at the Japs from the most desirable locations the guns had to be broken down again and moved by our mules to the selected areas. It was essential to zero them in on the hillside and on the Japanese who had our Second Battalion surrounded.

Two wheels for one of the guns were packed onto Jude and he carried the load easily. And again we 12 muleskinners were proud show-offs when we paraded back to our bivouac area with the mules and the guns.

Once the Howitzers were established at the desired locations no time was lost in firing their shells at the enemy surrounding Nhpum Ga; and the effect on both the Japanese and the Marauders was dramatic. The Japs, of course, were surprised when, for the first time, the heavy artillery fire they had been directing toward us was being returned. Moreover, we delivered a lot of fire toward the enemy in order to make the Japanese think we had more artillery than we actually possessed. Indeed, Jude and I were kept busy for a few days just carrying ammunition for the guns from the drop areas.

The heretofore sagging morale of the Marauders was restored significantly, even though the Japanese seemed to withstand our stepped-up artillery and strafing attacks along with the dropping of 500-pound bombs. But, there is no question that our new artillery fire, combined with the air attacks, had an impressive role in assuring the Marauders' final victory in the Nhpum Ga battle.

Jude and I continued our assignment of picking up an increasing number of airdrops from the Goony Birds and on one occasion we ran into a tragic situation. One of the C-47s made a different kind of noise when it came in for the drop and its crew kicked out supplies for us from the open door in the aircraft's fuselage. (Some of the planes had to make so many drops that their crews permanently removed the doors.) One of the parachutes opened before it was clear of the plane. As a result, the ropes hooked onto the tail section and badly damaged it, as well as creating so much drag that the airplane couldn't handle it. Consequently, the airplane crashed near our drop clearing, apparently killing all aboard. I never knew this for sure, because I was not part of the rescue team which rushed to the crash site. My assignment was to pick up the supplies that were scattered elsewhere and get them to their destination as soon as possible.

Meanwhile, of course, the Goony Birds also were making highly important drops of ammunition and supplies to the Second Battalion men trapped on Nhpum Ga Hill. They were vastly important. Not only did those men constantly need ammunition and food, but they also were cut off from the only fresh water hole that they had. However, this problem eventually was solved with typical American ingenuity. Our planes dropped heavy plastic bags filled with a total of some 500 gallons of water to the beleaguered men.

Yet, insufficient water and food were only part of the ordeal the men of the Second Battalion endured. Every time the Japs attacked by coming up the hill they suffered heavy casualties. Added to the bodies of some Americans, and of a number of their mules, the carcasses created an incredible stench throughout the area and attracted hordes of bluebottle flies. Sanitation problems were so severe that men with dysentery used their helmets as depositories for their excrement and kept them in some of the fox holes on the hill. We were relatively fortunate in the Hsamsingyang area. We were even able to wash our clothes in a nearby river and learned to do our laundry in the native style. We tied our fatigues in knots, slung them over our shoulders, and took them to the river where we hit them on the rocks in the stream's shallow shoals. We were still short on food, despite the airdrops. However, the K-rations were so highly concentrated that even after two or three bites they seemed to fill our shrunken stomachs and satisfy our cravings for hours to come. All in all, my only big worries at the time were running into Japanese ambushes or booby traps on the trips Jude and I made to the front lines, usually to carry more ammunition.

Eventually the decision was made to move the Howitzers closer to the Japanese positions on the hill. Naturally, Jude and I again were asked to help make the move and we willingly did so.

We heard one day that the Japs were bringing up more reinforcements from the south and the news caused us deep concern. But, the very next day we heard our enemies were weakening from the heavy casualties the Marauders were inflicting on them.

Sure enough, on the 12th day of the siege I was told to join a group of men with mules, stretchers, medical supplies and equipment bound for the hill. The Second Battalion had just been rescued by men from both the Third and First Battalions, the latter finally winning the battle at Shaduzup and reaching Nhpum Ga in a two-day march. Consequently, we could now take food and supplies directly to the long-beleaguered men.

My little party was the first among the rescuers to be sent to the top of the hill where the bitterest action had taken place. We found the scene there to be unimaginable. Japanese bodies were everywhere, supplemented by a relatively few corpses of Americans. Some mules also had been killed there and the stench from the bodies of both humans and animals simply was beyond belief. It was so bad that you wanted to fly away from the scene rather than staying to carry out your duties. There also was a dreadful impersonality about the scene. Death was such an overpowering presence that it was hard to remember that all of the bodies had once been living humans and animals.

The scene was made even more dismal by the hordes of so many blowflies buzzing around the bodies that their swarms sounded like airplane engines.

The first thing we had to do when we arrived on the battle-ground was to get the wounded who were still alive to a hospital as soon as possible, which meant that all of them would be flown back to Marghirita. I found one soldier who was able to sit up and ride on Jude while another was able to hold on to the side of my mule while we took both of them to a plane.

As I looked upon the battlefield scene, I could not help but wonder how nations and their leaders could ever decide that warfare was the way to settle their differences, and I was deeply saddened by the toll the Battle of Nhpum Ga had taken on the Marauders. While it was a good deal less than the number of casualties for the Japanese it nevertheless was substantial. Fifty-seven Marauders were killed, 302 wounded and 379 taken to a rear area hospital for treatment of malaria and dysentery, most of them returning to action later. But added to the casualties at Walawbum, where disease again was the main enemy, our original force of 3,000 men had dwindled to approximately 1800. And, the worst was still ahead.

Before leaving the story of the fighting at Nhpum Ga it is incumbent upon me to provide at least part of a more detailed and much more dramatic account of the battle that is contained in a remarkable narrative. It was put together by a number of surviving Marauders who cooperated in writing it. It is a devastating account of the Nhpum Ga struggle with the realism it brings into its combat descriptions, and never more so than in its story of the action at Nhpum Ga as follows:

"On March 25 the race was on to get out of the reach of the approaching Japanese and to dig in ahead of them at Nhpum Ga. The enemy was fresh and the Marauders were exhausted. The march to Nhpum Ga was almost more than the Marauders were able to endure either physically or psychologically. Actually, the 2nd and 3rd Battalions were going over much of the same territory they had just traveled. The round trip from Nhpum Ga to Inkangahtawng was 70 miles and the last 4 1/2 miles of the return trip was uphill and under very heavy enemy fire.

"One of the soldiers who was there described what those last few miles were like in the following manner: 'Move faster!' The call was passed up the line to men who were already exerting their last strength to force a shambling trot. The shells whinnied overhead and blasted the trail. There were more screams and moans from the injured, bringing home to the fleeing column its complete powerlessness. And as palpable as the steamy air for which the lungs labored was our awareness of the exultation of the enemy who thought they had us whipped. Yet the majority held fast. Men stopped and improvised litters for the maimed and struggled forward under the almost impossible loads. Medical corpsmen, answering calls for help, gritted their teeth and threaded their way back down the half-running column to bind up wounds and mount the casualties on horses. Muleteers, whose animals slipped and fell and slithered down the accursed inclines, dropped to their knees beside them and, wiping the sweat from their eyes, undid the buckles, got the packs off, fought the mules to a standstill, heaved the saddles back and laboriously reloaded.

"By 10:30 that morning, the bulk of the battalions had made it to Nhpum Ga. Some whose nerves had snapped were screaming into the aid station, which Major Rogoff had set up in the largest of the four bashas in the village. One man came into it shaking violently, tears streaming down his face. 'Major, I'm not afraid, damn it.' he cried. 'I tell you I'm not afraid. I just can't help shaking!'

"Men staggered up the last hill too exhausted to speak. One dropped in his tracks out cold. With the knowledge that there was no time to lose, the rest of the men commenced to prepare a perimeter along the lines marked out by Colonel McGee and his senior officers against the onslaught which they knew could not be long delayed.

"On March 28, the 2nd Battalion dug in at Nhpum Ga. The 3rd Battalion established a perimeter five miles farther north. In two days, the Japanese managed to surround and completely shut off the 2nd Battalion. Repeated attempts were made by the 3rd Battalion to reach them but each time they were turned back. The 2nd Battalion lost its only source of running water and for 10 days drank stagnant water and was under constant attack.

"In the meantime, the 1st Battalion had been ordered to go to the rescue of the 2nd and 3rd Battalions as quickly as possible. After a forced march of four days, mostly uphill, making only five or six miles a day, the 800 men of the 1st Battalion arrived at Nhpum Ga at 1700 hours on April 7. On the afternoon of April 6 the 1st Battalion had had a supply drop scheduled when it received the message that the 2nd and 3rd Battalions were in desperate need of support. So the men cancelled the drop at dark and, with empty stomachs and light packs, they moved out again and did not stop until midnight.

"Night marches were always difficult and seldom justified except in extreme circumstances. Unless the moon was at least half full the trail was impenetrable, as if one were moving with his eyes closed. The guides had to grope their way, and in an attempt to keep the rest of the column intact, the rest of the troops had to hang their respective compasses on the backs of the men or mules in front of them, and keep following close enough to keep the feeble glow of the dial in view. Those without compasses substituted pieces of decaying, phosphorescent wood picked up from the ground. Bivouacking in total darkness, with lights prohibited, required adaptability, especially when it was raining. The men of the 1st Battalion knew that they were a relief force and that their buddies' lives depended on them. Most of them carried large handkerchiefs cut from the rayon parachutes used for their supply drops and, wherever possible, the men used the color that corresponded with that of the name of the respective combat team. (The combat teams into which the battalion was divided were designated by colors, and four of the six were represented in the colors of the parachutes.) All up and down the long line of 800 men the colored handkerchiefs were broken out and tied around their necks as scarves. The last stage of the march was on fairly level ground so they were able to pick up speed a little, up to a three-mile -per-hour pace. No command was given to pick up the pace, it just happened. What a sight our men made in their mud-and blood encrusted uniforms, their faces drained white, dark circles under their eyes, many of them near exhaustion and one-third of them with dysentery. Yet that additional force of 800 men was all it took, and actually only 250 of them were fit enough to make an encircling movement the next day to free the 2nd Battalion. They arrived on a Friday afternoon, and by noon on Sunday, April 9, the 2nd Battalion was rescued and the Japanese were in retreat. It was a special day in more ways than one. It was an Easter Sunday."

I have another addendum to the Battle of Nhpum Ga, and it refers to Starkey and his 528th Dragonfly Squadron. It includes the following absorbing statistics. While supporting the Second and Third Battalions, the 528th's thirty P-51s flew 632 sorties, dropped 250 tons of bombs, and shot some 307,000 rounds of 50-caliber ammunition in support of the ground troops. Consequently, it is safe to say that the Marauders might well have lost the battle in which they were so heavily outnumbered by the Japanese if it had not been for the squadron's outstanding support. The squadron was given a post-war description by one of the Marauders of a bombing when a pilot dropped a 325pound depth bomb that burst in the tops of trees. He said that the blast "cleaned out the foliage, blew Japs out of their dug-outs, and we shot them in the air."

At the time of the Walawbum battle, the squadron was based in Assam Province in India and later moved to a base prepared for it at Tingkawk Sakan about 100 miles northwest from Myitkyina. After the Marauders captured the highly important airbase at Myitkyina the 528th flew hundreds of missions in support of the 85-day Marauder and Chinese siege of the town of Myitkyina itself. Finally, the squadron moved to China where it protected American airbases and the bombers stationed there.

My friend Starkey was one of the thirty members of the 528th"s "Century Club" composed of pilots who had flown more than 100 missions for the squadron.

Starkey, who was a personable and well-liked member of the squadron, also was known as one of its "characters". He was nicknamed 'Fingers' by his fellow aviators because he could find and eat PX rationed candy hidden by his squadron mates. On one of his takeoffs from the Tingkawk airstrip the propeller on his plane malfunctioned. The plane made a hard left turn and disappeared into the nearby jungle. Everyone was sure that 'Fingers' had "bought the farm" and they all ran into the jungle where the plane crashed, expecting to find a dead pilot in the wreckage. But here came Fingers walking back to the airfield and his first words were: 'Well, guys, I guess you want to hear my story.' He was right. They did!

The Value of Lives

There is no question that our enemies in The Great War often forgot the dignity and worth of each individual on the other side as well as on their own. To our Japanese foes in Burma this meant that they could torture American prisoners, belittle them, and even kill them with cruel and repugnant means.

We Americans displayed a great deal more humanity in our dealing with prisoners, although it must be noted that we seldom had any prisoners in Burma. Most of the Japanese preferred death to captivity and thus few of them were ever taken into our custody. In fact, there are several books written about the CBI theater which include photos of Japanese who had committed suicide rather than be captured alive. One of them shows a young Japanese soldier who had hung himself. Another, and even more inexplicable example of such self sacrifice on the part of the Japanese, is a photo showing at least 20 of them who had blown themselves up with a grenade inside a small basha hut.

Conversely, the Japs also demonstrated how cheaply they regarded the lives of others by the way they tortured and killed American, British, Chinese and Kachin prisoners. I've already described in this book how they treated Kachin captives in the Hukawng Valley, but they also treated British and American prisoners just as cruelly. Early in the war, when the Japanese were running the British out of southern Burma, they tied British prisoners to trees and used them for bayonet practice. Later on, some agents in the Americans' O.S.S. Detachment were in Lashio in Central Burma on one of their spying missions when they discovered that some of their friends had been captured and placed in a Lashio jail. Outside the jail they could hear their fellow agents screaming in agony as the Japanese tortured them.

They radioed out the news to an O.S.S. base and the Detachment's command asked American airmen to go to their rescue.

They flew planes directly over the jail and dropped bombs on it. The jail was blown to bits and O.S.S. Commander Ray Peers explained that his men had now been "placed beyond torture". Other O.S.S. agents operating in Rangoon, deep in Japanese held territory, were given poison capsules and told to use them if they were ever placed in danger of capture by the Japs. They ignored this counsel and suffered the consequences by being tortured to death.

Of course, the Japanese treatment of prisoners in Burma was no different than the treatment of American prisoners taken in the Philippines or the way they treated many of the civilian residents of Manila.

I have brought up the whole question of the treatment of prisoners to emphasize that the Americans were much more humane when they captured Japanese soldiers. I never heard of a single case of torture of a Japanese captive, although I knew of several who had been killed rather than taken as prisoners. There also were some instances of disrespectful treatment of the bodies of Japanese killed in their combat with us. One of those occurred very soon after the battle of Nhpum Ga. Some of our troops came upon the body of a large and red-headed Japanese soldier. They thought it was so unusual that they propped the body up against a tree as if the soldier were alive and resting there. Consequently, for the first time in our lives, those of us who saw the body were astounded to see a Japanese person with such unusual physical characteristics.

It required a few days of hard work to clean up Nhpum Ga Hill after the battle was over. Even the good feelings of at last being free of enemy fire in that bitter war were not enough to compensate for the sight of bodies of our fellow Americans, or for seeing so many wounded being prepared for evacuation. Even more disturbing was to witness at least a dozen American soldiers who had gone berserk. Apparently they were kept so busy during combat, and their attention so concentrated on staying alive, that they were able to retain their sanity until the action was over. Yet, afterward they found the continuing stench and the sight of bodies on Nhpum Hill so depressing that they finally "lost it". Consequently, I watched able-bodied and physically strong Americans screaming at the top of their lungs and literally trying to pull out their own hair. They, of course, were taken out of the regiment and sent to recuperate in rear area hospitals, although I have heard that some never regained their sanity, even after the war ended.

The approximate 1,800 men still on hand for combat in our regiment were only slightly more than half the number who had set out from India for our service with the Marauders. And the worst was yet to come. However, we did not know this and, therefore, all of our post-combat negative reactions were tempered for most of us by the good feeling that, at last, we must have been freed from any further combat duty in Burma; a mistaken notion it turned out, but one that gave us at least a temporary period of mythical relief.

I used this rest period to good advantage. Even Jude seemed to sense that he was able to get some respite from his long portage over the mountains and through the jungles on our journey from Assam. It was a change for him to have his daily ration of grain without having to quickly leave it and move on in order to dodge enemy fire; or seeing a delectable bamboo shoot that he had to leave untouched whenever I forced him to keep going down the trails. Instead, my faithful and long-suffering animal companion now basked in the attention I gave to him. This included the trimming of his mane and rubbing him down with a currycomb and brush. I also fed and exercised him on a regular schedule.

All of the mules were tethered to a picket line and each of us muleskinners took turns standing guard over them at night.

Our little interlude from combat was not completely without misery for me. I had watched dozens of my fellow soldiers laboring under the misery of amoebic dysentery, but my time did not materialize until we were resting from the battle at Nhpum Ga. However, when it came I knew it, and I had no trouble recognizing it. So, another soldier and I reported to a medic in a tent set up on the hill and he gave us some medicine and told us to rest for a few days. This we gladly did and our recovery was as prompt as it was welcomed.

Once in a while Jude and I also still had to go to dropping areas to recover food and supplies which were parachuted down to us by the Goony Birds. The second day after the end of the battle the planes dropped our first C-rations to us in place of the highly concentrated K-rations we had survived on during most of our march from Assam. The C-rations were a great improvement in taste, but our stomachs had shrunk so much that it required only a little food to satisfy our hunger. In fact, we were mistaken when we thought we were in for an exciting treat one day when some fried chicken and fried fruit pies were dropped to us. The same thing happened that occurred with the C-rations. Only a few bites were consumed and our stomachs were full.

It occurred to me one day during our rest period that I had not seen my friend Seymour Schoenfeld since we had left the Assam staging area several months previously. So I went to a tent where our headquarters company was located to see if there was any information about him there. Sure enough, a soldier clerk there found his name in the roster of the Khaki Combat Team of the Third Battalion, and the reason I had not seen him was that I had been serving in the Orange Combat Team. However, at this time his company was about a mile away from where I was located. Even so, I wasted no time hiking there to see if I could find him and hoping desperately that he was alive and well. I still could not forget that I had talked him into joining the Marauders, and I could only hope that he would not be holding it against me.

I need not have worried. I found him alive, in relatively good shape, and delighted to see me. However, we both had lost so much weight that, at first sight, we hardly recognized each other. We decided also that we had aged considerably since we had joined the Marauders and with good reason. We had aged a lot, both mentally and physically, since we had embarked on our great adventure.

We couldn't help but marvel at the fact that we had been so geographically close together ever since we came into Burma, and yet had never seen each other. We exchanged memories of the sinking of the Rohna as well as descriptions of the experiences in Burma we both had been through. He had heard about the dropping of the Howitzers from the airplanes; but he had no idea that Jude and I were selected to make one of the pickups and to take sections of these weapons to the site where they were put to such good use in helping the beleaguered Second Battalion. Schoenfeld, in turn, was assigned to a 60 mm mortar crew and had many close calls dodging enemy fire, but he never was wounded.

Finally, we shared our memories of the general at Fort Meade who had told us that "War is a killing game. Either kill or be killed." We agreed he was an astute individual and that I should have listened to his advice before I talked both Schoenfeld and myself into joining the Marauders.

When I left Schoenfeld, I hurried back to my own bivouac area because we were expecting an airdrop of great importance. It turned out that the drop was not made until the next morning, but it nevertheless was extremely well received. Everyone was given a new supply of clothes and shoes, along with food and regular supplies. As it turned out, we were informed that the drop was to be made closer to Schoenfeld's bivouac area than my own, so the next day I hurried down the trail to see him again, this time taking Jude with me. It felt like being in a different world when I received the new clothes and even got a haircut and shave from a battalion man who had been a barber in civilian life. Our old clothes were given to our Kachin guides who now were making patrols every day to be sure no Japanese troops would be sneaking up on us for a surprise attack. I made one Kachin very happy when I gave him the new pair of shoes I had received from the airdrop. I still preferred the fine paratrooper boots Starkey had given me when we arrived at Nhpum Ga. The Kachins also continued to be happy with the gifts we made to them of the parachutes used in the airdrops. They were made of the best cloth ever seen by our native friends and they used it to good advantage.

Our new clothing was issued just in time for us to look more presentable for an entertainment group that was coming in to put on a show for the regiment. The group was headed by screen actor Pat 0"Brien who demonstrated, in long conversations with us, that he really cared about the sacrifices we were making in the war. In this respect, he was much like fellow actor Melvyn Douglas who visited us when we were hiking down the Ledo Road. Thankfully, neither of them was like actress Ann

Sheridan. She came to India and Burma, quickly decided she didn't like the heat, diseases and other tough conditions of the CBI and so almost immediately returned to the states without meeting the terms of her USO commitment. The Marauders never even saw her during her brief visit to our little war zone.

Some years after the war, my collaborator in the writing of this book came across 0'Brien in a barbershop in the Pick-Congress Hotel in Chicago. When O'Brien learned that Hughes was a CBI vet who served in Burma he threw off his barber shop apron, jumped from his chair and came over to Hughes to engage him in a long conversation, his barber meanwhile waiting for him in order to finish his balding customer's haircut. When this cosmetic task finally was completed, O'Brien walked out of the shop yelling to everyone in the establishment, "The last time I saw that guy was in Burma".

THE ROAD TO MITCH

MITCH!

Every one of the English-speaking soldiers in Burma knew what and where Mitch was and why it was important in the war. Rangoon and Mandalay may have been more famous towns in Burma because of the stirring prose of Rudyard Kipling, but Mitch was the nickname for Myitkyina, and everyone in the Asian portion of the Great War knew where it was. They also knew why this obscure and relatively small village dominated the strategy of the American and Japanese forces in the north of Burma.

Mitch, the place that was located at the head of the Irrawaddy River with its water transportation system, as well as at the terminus of the north-south Burma railroads. Mitch, the site of a compacted gravel airstrip from which American planes would be able to fly the Himalayan "Hump" and keep China in the war with the supplies the Goony Birds transported into the western China metropolis of Kunming. Mitch, the site of the last desperate attempt by the Japanese to hold onto their north Burma conquests.

But we in the Marauders weren't too excited about the necessity of capturing Myitkyina. After all, we already had done more, much more, than we had been told we would have to do. We were now more than ready for Stilwell and other American commanders (all the way up to George C. Marshall) to keep their promises to us. Our ninety days service not only was more than completed but we had undertaken and won a devastating battle in which we never were supposed to have been involved. The Marauders were to have been the spearhead for the Chinese only long enough for Chiang's finest to get the head start we already had given them. Not to mention the fact that Chiang had more than 30 divisions in western China, a significant number of which, at any time, he could move into Burma to give us more assistance. (Myitkyina was very close to the western border of China and within easy distance for Chiang to transport a lot more of his troops.)

Therefore, after the bloody battle at Nhpum Ga, we were sure the promises to us would finally be kept and we would be rotated back to the states. And, Jude and I enjoyed our few days of rest. I was complacent that we would soon be backtracking the trails to Ledo and the India railway system which, in turn, would take us to the port at Bombay and the ship which would transport us home.

What fools we gullible mortals were. It wasn't long until we began to hear some disturbing reports that have been well-described by Charlton Ogburn in his book about the Marauders:

"A grotesque rumor began to be heard, passed along in deprecating tones, pretty much as a joke. The substance of the rumor was the possibility of our being sent against Myitkyina. It was entirely incredible, of course. We did not know how much farther we would have to walk to get to Myitkyina (about 90 miles) but we knew it was a damned long way over mountains higher and steeper than any we had crossed so far, and we knew it (Myitkyina) was the main (and well-manned) Japanese supply base in northern Burma with all that this implied.

"But incredible as the rumor was, it persisted, like a mosquito whining around your head.

'For Christ's sake, will you lay off that story!' Someone would explode. 'Are you asking for it?'

"It was like a tale of the supernatural in which, from a mere suggestion of something abnormal, a phenomenon of monstrous vitality and malignancy burgeons."

And, most unfortunately, the rumors turned out to be true.

The first thing that happened was a relatively short 30-mile hike, but a distance which required three days to traverse because of the thick jungle. However, we were headed back north, the direction from which we had come. This lent substance to our hope and belief that we were on our way home.

Moreover, when we arrived at the fairly large town of Naubum we learned that two regiments of the several divisions of Chinese troops promised by Chiang were indeed now on hand for any new offensive action and another was left behind to guard Nhpum Ga. Surely the use of our own regiment in any future operations would not be needed or wanted, especially since we had lost nearly half of our men and many still on duty were very sick.

However, it must be said that we were not very optimistic as to what the Chinese troops would be able to accomplish. Some of Lieutenant Ogburn's soldiers described the Chinese as "just a bunch of kids." Ogburn himself got the same impression when he went to their bivouac area to inspect them. Moreover, their record so far in our activity in north Burma indicated some disturbing weaknesses as well as a few strengths. They displayed as much courage and resolution when actually engaged in battle as did the Japanese. But the Chinese never wanted to get into combat conditions. Instead, they found the food, clothing and other benefits of military service (particularly with the help of American beneficence) to be so desirable that they wanted to keep enjoying those benefits with no risk to themselves. This applied to their field commanders as well. Up to this point, Stilwell and Merrill both had to keep pressuring these commanders to get them to advance against the Japanese.

In any event, our little period of recuperation and relaxation ended suddenly, and we not only felt like the axe had fallen, but that it was indeed taking off our heads. We were told that not only would we be on the march again, but that it would take us all the way over the dreaded Kumon Mountain range to Mitch. The only difference in our future blood, sweat and toil (we always decided we were too tough for tears) was that this time we would have some Chinese soldiers with us. Stilwell and Merrill decided that three different forces should be organized, the First and Third Battalions to be buttressed with one Chinese regiment for each of them and the Second Battalion to be strengthened by about 300 Kachins, which made the rest of us think how lucky the Second Battalion was; even though we in the other two battalions would have 3,000 Chinese soldiers each to help us. One Kachin, in our view, was worth ten Chinese any day. And subsequent developments demonstrated that we were right.

The two American-Chinese forces were designated as H Force for the First Battalion unit and K Force for my own Third Battalion unit. The Second Battalion unit with its Kachin troops was designated as the M Force.

The K Force and its Third Battalion, in which I was serving, was designated to take the lead in the initial phase of the march on Myitkyina. With the 88th Chinese Infantry Regiment tagging along, we were ordered to march on the village of Ritpong which was in Japanese hands on the other side of the 6,100-foot Naura Hkyat pass and about 30 miles to the southeast of our starting point. H Force would be spearheaded by the First Battalion, and buttressed by the 150th Chinese Regiment. It was to follow the K Force to Ritpong and, following its anticipated capture, would break to the southwest toward the village of Arang. K Force, in turn, would swing southeast toward Tingkrukawng. The two forces then would make a two-pronged swing back to the main trail where they would be joined by M Force consisting of some Marauders and 300 Kachin warriors. At that point the Marauders would have the Kumon Range behind them and would be poised for the last 60-mile advance to Myitkyina.

All of which appeared to be good planning and sound strategy. But, all of us in the ranks felt like this time we definitely had been betrayed and there was a sudden change among us in our attitudes and our morale. Up to this point we had confronted the ordeals of jungle combat with that cynical but nonetheless optimistic attitude toward the missions that were required of us. We griped constantly like soldiers always do, but when the time came to show our mettle we did so with courage and a fierce determination to conquer our detested enemies.

This time it was different, and the Marauders suffered a loss in morale which became more severe as we embarked on our third major mission. We faced the prospects of an even more difficult march than we had already experienced and the probability of still another tough battle at the end of our journey.

No longer did we engage in good-natured jabs at one another. No longer did we joke about what we would do to the Japanese when we came across a large force of them again. There was a subtle but nevertheless noticeable change in our attitudes. Those of us who had never fought in any previous combat before we came to Burma were affected more noticeably than the seasoned veterans who had participated in the Pacific island fighting. But you could sense that they, too, were emotionally disturbed by the way they swore at their officers and angrily went about the performance of their duties. All of us in the regiment felt we had been lied to on several occasions and that Joe Stilwell, nearly always ensconced safely in rear areas, had absolutely no concern as to whether we lived or died.

Our morale would have been even worse had it not been for a cagey decision by Colonel Hunter and one which future combat officers would be wise to emulate. In order to keep us from brooding at our jumping off place at Hsamshingyang, he amazingly ordered us into some close order drill, ordinarily an activity which soldiers fiercely want to avoid. But this time it helped to keep us from brooding and rebuilt our pride in the Marauders as a unit. It would be hard to explain the feelings we experienced when we started to count in cadence so loudly that we must have scared away every animal prowling the nearby jungle. We were American soldiers, By God, and more than that, we were the Marauders who had been tested and not found wanting in the challenges and ordeals of combat against our enemy.

Just before we left the Nhpum Ga area I visited again with my pal Schoenfeld and we pledged to keep in touch with each other for the rest of our lives.

Let me now deal for a minute with the Kumon Range and the enormous challenge it presented in our march to Myitkyina.

You will find no mention of the Kumon Mountains even in the largest encyclopedias. But when Winston Churchill said at Quebec that the Marauders would have to fight their way over the world's most forbidding terrain he must have been thinking about the Kumon range. It was not that the height of these mountains was as great as those of other formidable mountains in the world. Indeed, the nearby Himalayan range far exceeded the Kumons in altitude. But, the Kumons had extremely steep grades to climb and they were covered with some of the densest and most dangerous jungle growth to be found anywhere. Additionally, the air was full of every kind of hostile and disease bearing insect known to man, not to mention unfriendly beasts of prey ranging from tigers to such extremely poisonous members of the serpent family as cobras and kraits. At one point, several Americans in our force thought they were stepping on some logs when they were pushing a mule out of some mud. But, one of the logs suddenly moved and it was discovered it wasn't a log after all. Rather it was a 20-foot python that thankfully decided not to wrap himself around one of the soldiers and crush him to death in the manner of both its species and boa constrictors. Instead, it slithered off into the jungle while the Marauders cheered its departure.

However, the two worst enemies to the Marauders were heavy rains and huge elephant leeches which dwarfed even those we had found in the Patkai Mountains and the Hukawng Valley. Some of us appeared to be moving fountains of blood which had discolored our clothing to a dark red. The leeches seemed to be everywhere in the jungle, and many of them dropped off on us from the leaves on bamboo trees.

The rain was almost constant and seemed even to exceed the drenching we had received in Assam. Moreover, it caused all of us more misery than we suffered from any of the other conditions we experienced in the Kumons. First, it was so constant that we never experienced a day without it. Secondly, since it rained both day and night, we never found any use for the soggy blankets we had been carrying up to that point. Instead, we each kept two waterproof ponchos we used every night. One was employed to cover each of us and the other to place on the soaking wet ground beneath us.

But, the worst result of the monsoon rains was the mud it created on the almost invisibly small trails we were following. The trails were also known only to our Kachin guides. I found it more difficult to traverse these trails on the uphill grades, although the slippery downhill slopes could be treacherous, particularly for those of us who were leading mules. However, it was even tougher going on the uphill grades because they required more of our dwindling strength and endurance, as well as creating as much hazard from slippery footing as did the downhill slopes.

Imagine, if you will, the kind of challenges we faced when, on one occasion, we climbed from an altitude of approximately

1,300 feet to over 6,000 feet in less than a half mile of forward movement, all of it in mud and, in my case, tugging a mule along behind me. And every day proved to be tougher than the preceding one. For example, we managed to march some 26 miles over the foothills on the first day of our odyssey, but when we hit the higher altitudes it required five days to traverse a 15-mile distance.

As Charlton Ogburn put it in his book about the Marauders: The experience "was so bad it was preposterous". The only thing that kept the Marauders going, Ogburn believed, was the feeling that each moment was the worst of all and that nothing ahead could be as bad.

Ogburn also had a special feeling for us muleskinners and our animals and all that we went through. He has described our ordeal in these words:

"The saw-toothed ridges would have been difficult to traverse when dry. Greased with mud, the trail that went over them was all but impossible. On the steeper descents, the mules simply sat down, sliding 50 yards or more on their haunches. Going up, we hacked steps out of the steeper slopes to give them a foothold.

"The battle of the mules was unending and, I think, took more out of the men than anything else, more even than fighting the enemy and fighting disease. When the mules slipped and fell, which they did continually under their heavy loads, there was, as always, the man-killing labor of getting them unloaded, staggering up the hills with the components of the cargo, and reloading them. The mule leaders became virtually dehumanized.

"The worst of it was when the mules, losing their footing, would be toppled off the trail altogether and go head over heels down the Mountainside or stabbing themselves with bamboo. One day, in a stretch of only a few miles, the Third Battalion lost twenty of its mules, which meant not only the mules themselves, but about two tons of supplies, weapons and equipment."

Ogburn, if anything, understated rather than overstated the case. I saw five mules go over the ridge on one day alone, falling one right after another at a particularly bad spot in the trail.

And then I lost Jude.

We were going up a steep incline when Jude and another mule started sliding, could not regain a foothold, and went over the edge of a high cliff. Without his surgically removed voice box Jude could make no complaint and he simply fell to the bottom of the cliff where the dense jungle hid him from my sight.

And with Jude went the last thing that had made life in Burma bearable for me. It may seem strange that an intelligent and normally realistic human being would lose touch with reality to the extent that a mule became one of his very best friends. But it truly was a fact and for these reasons: Jude and I were hardly ever apart from each other ever since we had left Assam. Moreover, during the daylight hours the two of us usually were separated from the other soldiers and animals on that long trail. Consequently, since I always have been a loquacious person, I found Jude was the only living being I could talk to during a difficult journey when communication of any kind could make you forget your troubles, and the fact that Jude couldn't answer me made little difference. In my civilian life I was used to talking a lot more than listening. Moreover, I sensed that Jude was responding to me even though he could not talk or even bray. When things got hectic during our frequent battles or skirmishes I could almost always manage to keep him calm. I could make him hurry on the trail or slow him down. In fact, he was generally a compliant animal, for a mule, and he would respond to nearly all of my commands to him. And I reiterate that, more than anything or anyone else, Jude had always been in my presence. We simply were never apart. As a result, I immediately felt something missing on the trail when he was no longer around.

Little did I know that I soon would not even be able to communicate with my army comrades at the nighttime bivouacs. Indeed, I was to learn what complete loneliness was, and how it felt to feel a separation from every living thing on earth except those creatures that were hostile to you. And, it was a true miracle in every sense of the word that I managed to survive.

Lost in the Jungle

It is perhaps no exaggeration to say that a number of Marauders became the "walking dead" on the long road to Mitch. And I was one of them.

As mentioned previously, our regiment, with its original 3,000 men, had been cut to about half that size after the Battle of Nhpum Ga. We suffered more fatalities from disease than from combat, and by the time we were on the road to Mitch there was hardly any Marauder who did not have at least one kind of jungle illness. In my case I was suffering from both malaria and amoebic dysentery (later to be compounded by typhus fever) and I could barely stand erect, much less make any forward movement on the trail. I also had no alternative to staying on the trail since the medics required 105-degree fevers three days in a row before you could be evacuated to a rear area hospital. But I was to learn that this standard had been set too high, at least in my case.

Eventually, after about 15 days on the trail (and shortly after I lost Jude) I finally had to sit down and rest while the column of men continued its forward march. When I tried to rise again, I passed out. When I regained consciousness I was confused and I wandered off the trail and into the jungle where no one else among both the Americans and Chinese in our column could see me. Then I apparently lost consciousness again, regained it again, and wandered farther into the jungle. By this time the sun was going down and a short time later I found myself lost in the jungle in total darkness.

For the next four days I wandered in a dazed condition during the daylight hours and, I must admit, slept rather fearfully during the night, sometimes getting no sleep at all. I had K-rations to eat, but my stomach by this time had shrunk so much I could hardly swallow them.

During the daylight hours, I tried to find my way back to the trail and followed the sound of gunfire I heard in the distance. But I had no luck and instead found myself one day just a few feet below a huge python snake resting in a tree above me. Such serpents seldom attack humans, especially if their world's longest stomachs are full and they are resting. But if they are hungry, restless and on the move they can be very serious trouble. Thankfully this one appeared to be well sated and wasn't interested in me. Nevertheless, I wasted no time getting away from him, or her, whichever the case had been.

I received a much bigger and more serious scare the next day.

I was still conscious only part of the time and, on this occasion, had somehow fallen into a foxhole that the Japanese apparently had dug in the jungle. How long I lay there unconscious I do not know, but I'll never forget the sensation I had when I awoke and looked up into the top of a bamboo tree about 20 yards away from me. There, looking down on me with his bright feline eyes, was a large, black panther. I still had enough of my wits about me that I didn't try to break and run, running being impossible for me anyway in the condition I was in. So I lay in the foxhole as quietly as I could and neither the panther nor I made a move. Finally, after about half an hour of the stand-off, I climbed out of the foxhole and quietly stole away. To this day I still thank the good lord that the panther made no move to follow me or to jump on me.

I lost all track of time and the eerie solitude of the jungle was getting on my nerves. And, as always, I was constantly a victim of mosquitoes and leeches who seemed to adore the taste of my blood.

My tactic of following the sound of gunfire during the times when I was able to move did not prove to be helpful. I knew that I was more likely to run into friendly troops than the enemy's since the Marauders ostensibly were between the Japanese and me. The gunfire kept sounding farther away which correctly indicated to me that the Marauders were pushing the Japs further south and east in the drive toward Myitkyina. But, the action must have moved forward so rapidly that I was left farther and farther behind. Meanwhile, I didn't take chances on coming across a stray Japanese scout or an entire patrol, inasmuch as that had become a frequent occurrence for our own scouts during our entire trek from Shingbwiyang. Indeed, I kept coming across abandoned Japanese foxholes in which I would stay during the night's hours, covering myself with large banana leaves to escape detection. (They sometimes grew to a length of ten feet or more and most of them also were wide enough to cover my body.)

It never occurred to me that I would be rescued in the manner that I was, or that my rescuer would not be a Marauder, but rather one of the blessed Kachins. However, I should have known it would be one of them who would find me. In addition to their highly effective ambush tactics against the Japanese, the Kachins also had achieved a reputation for rescuing numerous American airmen who had crashed in the jungle. (After the war the story was related in several books about the experience of one airman, identified as a Lieutenant MacFarland, who crashed in the jungle and who, like me, had spent four days in the wilds. He kept thinking that some Japanese were chasing him when, in reality, it was a party of Kachins. Finally, one Kachin caught up with him and he was carrying a large placard on which was printed the message 'Lt. Jenkins and Lt. MacFariand follow this man.' MacFariand did so and was guided by the Kachin back to an American base. Lt. Jenkins had been picked up by a Third Battalion patrol on the preceding day.)

And so it was that on my own fourth day in the wilderness, I saw a man in a T-shirt and ragged shorts who had a brown skin and was barefooted. He was wearing a U.S. army cap and was carrying a machete as his only weapon. He was, in other words, a cheerful, buoyant and carefree Kachin. Along with several others, he had been assigned to patrol the jungles along the march to Myitkyina for the precise purpose of locating and leading to safety any GIs who became lost in the wilds. He could speak no English but indicated by sign language that I was to follow him. I did so for the next eight to ten hours until we reached the bivouac of some Chinese soldiers who had a few American soliders with them.

But we no sooner had arrived there than I was a reluctant witness to a bizarre and revolting incident.

I already had been apprised of the harsh discipline that was rampant in the Chinese army. Whenever a soldier in the ranks committed an offense, no matter how minor, his officers did not bother with a reprimand, confinement or hard labor. Instead, he was immediately executed. Moreover, the offenders seemed to expect such treatment and it still did not deter them from committing infractions that would result in their deaths.

It was on my third day at the bivouac when I saw five Chinese soldiers digging a trench in the muddy and soft Burma soil. The trench ended up being about ten feet long and three feet wide and another five soldiers were supervising the diggers' labor.

No one was angry and both groups of men appeared to be happy. Smiles appeared on the faces of all of them and good-natured banter was being exchanged. The cheerful faces of the men who were digging the trench particularly struck me and, indeed, I was impressed by how willingly they were going about their labor. But, a short while later, I could not comprehend how they could have maintained such a demeanor.

When they had completed the digging, they still had smiling and carefree expressions on their faces as the other five soldiers commanded them to stand in front of the trench. Then, stationed about 15 feet away, the executioners opened fire with their Springfield rifles. Their marksmanship was excellent and one shot each was all it took to kill the victims, all of whom either fell backward into the trench or subsequently were shoved into it.

Ever since that appalling incident occurred I have wondered about my own reaction to it. I have always considered myself compassionate and I have placed great value on human life. I have never favored capital punishment, even for serious crimes.

And yet, I had absolutely no reaction to the executions I witnessed at that time and place in Burma. Why? I am not quite sure, but I suspect it was because of the conditioning I received in Burma. First, I had grown accustomed to seeing death in all forms and at times when it was a daily occurrence. I also had seen the habitual brutality of Chinese officers in the way they treated their troops. Finally, I had learned what little value the Chinese soldiers themselves placed on their own lives. They were accustomed to extreme poverty and the very lowest of living conditions.

Furthermore, they had long been subjected to war and combat conditions, first in the Japanese attacks on China and, secondly, in the constant internal strife between the nationalist and communist forces in China. Consequently, they had grown to believe that life had little value to them and they anticipated that their superior officers would hold the same assumption toward them when it came to punishment for any misdeeds.

THE FALL OF MYITKYINA

Some American liaison officers at the Chinese bivouac informed me that the Marauders and the Chinese now had the Japanese on the run and that little opposition remained on the last remaining miles to Myitkyina. The bivouac was a short distance away from Ritpong which was captured easily by H and K Forces, both of which were reunited with M Force a short distance south of the village, with about another sixty miles remaining on the trail to Mitch. But the cost of taking Ritpong was high. Sanitary conditions of the Japanese occupying force were extremely bad. As a result, typhus-bearing fleabites were rampant among our troops and caused a substantial number of them to succumb to the dread disease. I therefore congratulated myself on not being in Ritpong, but I did so prematurely, as it turned out.

The liaison officers kindly gave me some parachutes on which to sleep and I found them to be much more comfortable than my wet poncho. After a three-day rest at the Chinese encampment, my Kachin guide led me on a half-day's hike south to the headquarters of the aforementioned Colonel Charles N. Hunter. Hunter was now second in command of the Marauders' regiment and he twice succeeded General Merrill as the commanding officer when Merrill suffered a pair of heart attacks, first at Nhpum Ga and later at Myitkyina. Hunter was an outstanding officer who wrote a scathing post-war denunciation of General Stilwell in a book Hunter published under the title of GALLAHAD, the secret code name devised for the Marauders' mission at the Roosevelt-Churchill Quebec Conference.

Hunter's headquarters was modest to say the least, his 'office' being a medium-sized tent in still another bivouac area. I was still too sick to perform any duties and for several days suffered the misery of dysentery and a high fever. Finally, on the day before the Marauders easily captured the Myitkyina airstrip, the officers there decided I was sick enough to be evacuated to the 14th Evacuation Hospital in Assam and I was sent there in a small L-5 liaison plane. The doctors there diagnosed my illnesses as being amoebic dysentery and the non-cerebral type of malaria, and they started me on a course of treatment. After a week of treatment I felt a little better, although I still was confined to bed most of the time. I later was to learn what had happened to the Marauders after I was hospitalized. A total of about 1,300 men, less than half our original strength, were still in action when the regiment arrived at the Myitkyina airstrip, after having lost at least 100 men each day due to diseases incurred or having reached the critical state during the ordeal of crossing the Kumon range. Yet, the remainder of the regiment captured the airfield with surprising ease, discovering only a few Japanese in its vicinity.

This exhilarated General Stilwell to such an extent that he immediately flew himself and a contingent of prominent American newsmen to Myitkyina for coverage of this "great victory." He not only was premature, but he refused to reply to Colonel Hunter's question as to whether his forces should proceed to capture the town of Myitkyina itself which was located about four miles away from the airstrip. Hunter never learned why Stilwell failed to give him instructions at that time, but he guessed it was because Stilwell wanted to confer with General Merrill before making that decision. But Merrill, in turn, had told Hunter not to worry about any instructions he was to receive until he, Merrill, arrived at the strip. However, as soon as Merrill did so he suffered his second heart attack in Burma and had to be evacuated to a rear area hospital.

No one worried too much about any need to hurry in launching the attack and for an interesting reason. Hunter had been assured by Stilwell that the town was occupied by only a few hundred enemy troops, information which had been given the general by his intelligence officer who, in an interesting case of nepotism, happened to be Stilwell's son and namesake, Colonel Joseph W. Stilwell, Jr.

Actually, it was learned later that a much higher number of Japanese soldiers were in the town and more were being brought in from Mogaung only a short distance away, their number eventually reaching more than four thousand. In the absence of this information, Hunter finally decided he had to make the decision himself and started an attack on the town.

This situation grew into one of the two largest and fiercest battles to be fought in Burma, the other being the British victory over the Japanese divisions at Imphal in eastern India. And for this battle, Stilwell had made no preparations at all, including the sending of urgently needed reinforcements into the area. Instead, he made a decision that caused the most unforgivable controversy of the Burma war. He ordered doctors to pull everyone out of the evacuation hospital who could get out of bed and walk in order to help him rectify the mistake he had made in not ordering an attack earlier on the town. Consequently, some 200 Marauders were yanked out of their hospital beds and sent back to the front. I was one of them and to this day I still hold a deep and abiding grudge toward a man whose so-called achievements in Burma resulted in his promotion to the rank of a full general, becoming one of only four at that time to hold such an exalted status in the entire United States Armed Forces. Stilwell never denied making the decision to send hospitalized soldiers back into combat, but he later claimed that his instructions had been 'misinterpreted' by the officers who came to the hospital and yanked us out of it. In fact, one report had it that Stillwell wept when he learned what had been done, but that report was ludicrous. Vinegar Joe was not the crying kind. Moreover, he already had shown complete disregard for his soldiers' lives when he periodically went into the field and saw what they were going through and yet made no move to send in additional men to help them — some 100,000 noncombatant troops (including the collaborator in writing this book) being stationed at that time in India, many of whom could have been sent into combat. And, in fact, Stilwell finally made a belated decision to send in as replacements at Myitkyina the members of two combat engineer battalions who were still working on the construction of the

Ledo Road. Additionally, Stilwell could have called on thousands of rear echelon and/or administrative units in India to help out in what truly was an emergency situation. After all, history is replete with combat actions in which such reinforcements were successfully utilized. But, instead, the dwindling elements of the worn-out and by then demoralized Marauders were still being forced to bear all the burden of combat for more than a month after the airstrip was captured and in the subsequent attack on the town itself. The help they were supposed to get from the Chinese regiments proved abortive at that point. On one occasion during the march to Myitkynia, the Chinese mistakenly shelled a detachment of Marauders near the town of Ritpong. Later, in the siege of Myitkyina, a Chinese regiment spent one night firing all of the ammunition into the air that had been flown into them the previous day. Later, two Chinese battalions were sent out one afternoon during the siege, lost their way, and mistakenly started firing on each other, causing numerous casualties. On the very next afternoon this blunder was repeated with an even larger number of casualties. Still later, a Chinese regiment managed to fight its way into the outskirts of Myitkyina before it panicked and hastily withdrew under withering Japanese fire.

Nevertheless, the Chinese on various occasions demonstrated their courage once they were under fire. And like some of the cavalry units of the American Wild West, they always started a charge with the blowing of bugles. Additionally, the Chinese were willing to fight with the cold steel of bayonets whenever it became necessary.

The toll for the Marauders in capturing the town of Myitkyina was higher than in any previous engagement in which we had fought. In this action, some 272 Americans were killed and 955 were injured. Moreover, it left less than 300 Marauders still able to fight out of the total of 3,000 which had set out from the town of Ledo in Assam some ten months earlier.

When I was sent back to Myitkyina from the hospital, I was still so weak that I was assigned only to the carrying of messages from headquarters to officers at the front where the battle was being fought. However, even that relatively easy responsibility proved to be too much for me when my fever starting an upward climb again and I grew so weak that I could not stand upright. I learned why this was happening when, after only a few days at Myitkyina, I was sent back to the evacuation hospital. And not too soon, it turned out. Doctors there quickly discovered that, on top of malaria and amoebic dysentery, I was now also suffering from typhus fever that developed when my resistance already had been seriously weakened. My future at that point depended figuratively on a toss of the dice. Some of the Marauders who had come down with it during the battle at Ritpong contracted what is identified in medical textbooks as the Epidemic Louse-Borne Typhus that is fatal in up to 80 per cent of the people contracting the disease. But others developed the less serious but nevertheless crippling variety known as the Marine Flea Borne Typhus and I luckily had fallen victim to it.

Nevertheless, I was bedridden with a fever that kept on getting higher, and I was losing a substantial amount of weight, the scales showing I was now down to less than 100 pounds. For a while, I was deeply despondent, but I also kept feeling better physically and counted myself lucky. I figured that anyone who, in the space of ten days, could get lost in one of the world's worst jungles in a semiconscious condition, stumble into interesting situations with a python and a black panther, and then fall victim to three potentially fatal diseases, had to count himself quite fortunate to still be among the living.

But, I remained weakened to the extent that the doctors insisted on keeping me in the hospital for a solid month.

On top of this fortunate development, (which kept me out of any further danger at Myitkyina) I was then flown with several other soldiers to a rest camp near Calcutta. I never had dreamed that this dismal city could now seem so heavenly to me. The famine in Bengal Province, by now, had ended and I stumbled into an incredibly fortunate situation at the rest camp. Whom did I see once again but my old buddy Schoenfeld? The two of us kept abreast of the events at Myitkyina through conversations with others who kept arriving at the convalescence center. By this time, so many Marauders were caving in from diseases and their long ordeal that only about 300 (less than one-tenth of our original strength) remained to help carry forward the efforts with the Chinese and the Combat Engineers to capture the town of Myitkyina. After more than a month of fighting, they finally were successful and thereafter there occurred a big "turkey shoot". The dwindling Japanese survivors got on rafts and tried to float down the Irrawaddy River to join Japanese forces who were charged with the assignment of defending the towns of Bhamo and Lashio, both of them a relatively short distance away from Kipling's storied city of Mandalay. But it was an abortive flight. Americans, Kachins and Chinese all lined up along the banks of the river and shot down many of the fleeing Japanese.

Army statistics revealed that the fighting at Myitkyina again was very costly to our enemy. An estimated total of 790 Japanese were killed and some 1,180 were wounded.

When the fighting ended, a relatively small number of surviving Marauders were evacuated from Myitkyina; but then they went berserk and effectively damaged the up-to-then commendable reputation of the regiment. They had been sent to a convalescence camp near Marghirita in Assam where conditions were quite deplorable. There were no buildings in the usual sense, just some make-believe bamboo structures. They had dirt floors, which were a far cry from the gleaming and polished concrete floors of today's modern hospitals. Heavy monsoon rains, combined with excessive heat such as only Assam could generate, made the patients despondent and very angry when combined with the other conditions with which they were coping. They were also enraged by the broken promises Stilwell and his staff had made to them.

Somehow a group of them found some beer, as well as a highly intimidating concoction from the Assam tea plantations known as "Bullfight Brandy" and they proceeded to run amok. After terrifying nurses and tearing up medical officers' quarters, they went on a spree one night which ended with the destruction of their own canteen. It was this episode which led to a lot of unfavorable publicity about the Marauders in stateside newspapers and nearly ruined the reputation they had achieved as a most valorous fighting unit.

I had similar reasons to be disgruntled, but I confined myself to meditating a great deal about the terrible cost in lives and mutilation that the Marauders had endured all the way from Ledo to Myitkyina, not to mention the action which was to follow the capture of Myitkyina. All told, official statistics at the end of the war disclosed that 97 Marauders were killed in battle, 30 died from diseases, eight were missing in action, and 383 were wounded. Just as interesting were the additional numbers of men who were so incapacitated by diseases that they could not be returned to battle. For example, the adjutant general of the American armies provided the following figures on Marauders who were hospitalized at three different rear area hospitals during the war with the identities of the diseases from which they suffered: Amoebic dysentery 503, scrub typhus 140, malaria 203, psycho-neurosis 72 and miscellaneous 930, most of whom were suffering from several different diseases. Of the approximately 2,600 Marauders who actually entered combat a total of 2,394 were lost from one cause or another.

All of this was in sharp contrast with the more acceptable statistics of the Marauders' combat action after the fall of Myitkyina. And small wonder. This time we were part of a 100,000-man force instead of a 3,000-man regiment. We became part of the recently arrived 475th Infantry Regiment of American soldiers. It was incorporated into the newly-named "Mars Task Force" which also included the American 124th Cavalry Regiment (which actually served on foot), four Chinese divisions, and the British-Indian 36th Division.

Would that we Marauders had been given all that support in our drive from Ledo to Myitkyina! But the Marauders' regiment now had been deactivated, and most of its soldiers had been sent home to the blessed, the wonderful, the heavenly United States.

Those who went home were mainly the men who previously had served in the South Pacific and thus had accumulated enough points under the newly devised point system to receive priority for discharge and their return to the States. The highest number of points were garnered by those who were married, had children, had the longest service in the military, and who had served the longest time overseas.

Unfortunately for me, I was married, had no children, and had only a year's service in the army, most of the time in the States. Consequently, I was one of the very few men in the Second and Third Battalions who had to remain in Asia, together with a group of about twenty in the First Battalion. But hey, this time I lucked out. Both Schoenfeld and I were sent to Bhamo, a village some distance south of Myitkyina, and I learned upon my arrival that I would be assigned some clerical duties at the Mars Task Force headquarters. Talk about a contrast with what I had experienced in the preceding few months! My new comrades at Bhamo had to keep correcting me when I said I had been treated to an early arrival in paradise. I was now eating cooked food off tables and sleeping on a cot under a tent. Additionally, I could listen to entertaining music on an American army radio station. And when the army diet got monotonous for any of us we simply would throw a hand grenade into the Irrawaddy River to kill fish and cook them in a helmet along with rice. All of this seemed like heaven compared with the experiences we Marauders had survived in the Burma jungles and mountains.

I was assigned to the headquarters of the First Battalion, 475th Infantry Regiment, and found life to be much easier behind a typewriter than in front of a mule on a jungle trail. Moreover, I was given an interesting duty that arose from a bizarre and unfortunate incident on the Marauders' punishing hike over the Kumon Mountain range toward the end of the regiment's march across Burma. The regiment's personnel files and other records were carried by a mule who, along with others, fell to his death from a high cliff. He tumbled so far down the slope in such heavy underbrush that all efforts to find both the animal and the records failed. Consequently, it now became my job to reconstruct these records and also prepare a list of all members of the Marauders who were entitled to the Combat Infantry Man's badge, one of the most coveted awards in all of America's military forces.

To re-create the personnel records was not an easy task. We obtained information and copies of records on each Marauder from a number of sources, and eventually we were able to put together a good deal of information on both the men still alive and those who died for their country in the Burma war. It was interesting work and I felt it made an important, if small contribution to the men still alive and to the families of those who were deceased.

I remained at Bhamo for about six weeks while the Mars Task kept pushing farther south in Burma, eventually reaching the place where the Ledo Road could be connected to the Burma Road, a happy event which enabled a significant increase in the transportation of weapons and supplies eastward into China.

Then Schoenfeld and I (still remarkably being able to stay together) were flown several hundred miles to the east to the large city of Kunming, China, where the Mars Task Force was given a new assignment, namely to help protect American air bases which the Japanese were starting to overrun. In fact, they captured and managed to maintain control for a brief time over the bases at Liuchow and Kweilin east and south of Kunming.

While soaring over the towering Himalayan mountains toward Kunming I was told by a crewmember in my plane that our aircraft didn't really need a navigator. When I asked why this was true, particularly in a flight over an enormous mountain range, I was told to look out the window. When I did I saw numerous wrecked American airplanes. Japanese aircraft had shot down some of them, but most of them had crashed in the severe weather of Asian monsoons in mountain country where, even in good weather, the wind and turbulent air were enough to send a plane out of control.

Navigation, however, soon became an easy chore.

"All we have to do is follow the wreckage of those planes," the crewmember told me. "The trail they make can lead us all the way to Kunming." I later learned that it had been given the nickname "The Aluminum Trail."

My situation in Kunming was even better than it was in Bhamo. I was assigned to good living quarters and the 475th headquarters office was located in what passed for a quality brick building in the China of those years. We had clean bathrooms (a real rarity in the Asia of that time) and waiters served meals to us. But the work got tougher and more time consuming. I toiled far into the night seven days a week and still needed more hours to catch up on securing all the necessary information for adequate personnel files on the Marauders.

I enjoyed the work but I also was getting impatient to return to the United States; three officers and seventeen enlisted men of the remaining Marauders at Kunming shared that sentiment.

Consequently, I agreed to send a letter in behalf of our group to General Merrill who appeared to be the only individual who could go to bat in our support. Sent on May 28, 1945, the letter said in part that we unfortunately were victims of the army 'point system' that was being used to determine the order in which men would be sent home. This system had nothing to do with the time soldiers spent in combat but, instead, was heavy on such considerations as length of service in the army and the number of family dependents claimed by each man. I regarded this as a form of discrimination against the soldiers who had endured the most hardships and made the greatest contributions and sacrifices in the war against the Japanese. I pointed out that, in my case, I had spent 20 of my 25 months in the army overseas, which was a much greater proportion than that served by many of the men already sent home. I did not mention, although I should have, that we in the Marauders also had endured hardships that were greater than those inflicted upon most of our soldiers in the Great War. Perhaps most unfairly of all, we at Kunming were victims of an administrative decision which ruled that, because we arrived in CBI in October of 1943 instead of the previous month of September, we were not eligible, like many of the other Marauders, to have already been sent home in April of 1944. Those men had only 14 more days of overseas service than we did but, because of that lonely fact, they were sent home early and we in Kunming had to remain there indefinitely because of our small deficiency in the 'point system.'

General Merrill's response, when it came, was hardly satisfactory. He said in his letter to us that some of the rear area administrative and service troops were disgruntled that their departure for home was delayed because they felt that 'we were giving too many breaks to the combat troops.' He then followed that less-than-reassuring statement with this ringing declaration: "I'm really sorry I can't help you and I have given you an honest answer. Whatever you think about me on this deal at least give me credit for not handing you a line of bull about "There is still a big war out here to fight." Please show this to all the others interested because I will go nuts if I have to answer another letter giving so much detail.'

Needless to say, we did not impose upon our old commander with any other letters which might send him nuts. But then a miracle occurred. Orders were received on June 4 ordering all of us still at Kunming to be transported by the first available transportation by land or by sea to the United States. Whether General Merrill was instrumental in arranging this happy event for us we never did learn before his sudden and untimely death back in the states. But I am sure that my letter to him reminded him that he should somehow communicate to his Marauders his appreciation for our service in Burma. On June 7, only a few days after my missive was sent to him, he wrote and mailed a very fine letter to all of the surviving Marauders whose addresses he could find and which read in part as follows:

"I want everyone to know that I feel that I have been very fortunate, and more so than any other commander in this war, to have had the opportunity of commanding (the) 5307th. All of you know what you have accomplished and I will not waste time on this.

However, I want you to know that I feel that no other outfit in the United States Army could have accomplished the work which you have done."

In very short order those of us at Kunming packed our duffel bags and boarded a plane which took us back to Calcutta and the same tent city to which I had been sent upon my arrival in India. And the surroundings were no more pleasant than they had been before. Moreover, I was then subjected to what may have exceeded even the discontent we had experienced in the days and months of the Burma war. After all the hardship, after all the danger, and with all the expectations of being sent HOME again, we spent six long weeks in the heat and discomfort of the tent city waiting for that "first available transportation" to show up.

Finally, to heap still more resentment upon us, we were not given the rapid and comfortable air transportation back to the states that most of our other comrades in the regiment and thousands of the rear area troops had received. Instead, we were given the same kind of trip home that we received when we traveled to Asia, namely another 30-day boat ride over virtually the same route as the one we followed on our trip to the CBI theater. The only difference was that we sailed out of the Calcutta seaport into the Bay of Bengal and the Indian Ocean and around the southern tip of India before we headed north and west to reach Bombay. But after we left Bombay we followed the same course as before, sailing north on the Arabian Sea into the Red Sea and the Mediterranean Sea and thence west on the Atlantic Ocean to the port at New York. And yes, you guessed it, Schoenfeld and I were still together and we were able to keep in close touch with each other until his death in 1995.

But we parted in New York and it appeared that even after hitting the North America continent I was to be given the longest possible trip home. At New York I was put on a train that went north into Canada before heading due west. Then it re-crossed the border and headed due west again before reaching Chicago. At that point, after riding both a boat and a train, I was put on a bus to head south and to my HOME in Missouri.

I came home to a nation at peace again, V-J Day occurring while I was on the Indian Ocean. Did I kiss the ground when I arrived back in the states? You bet I did, and at every stop made by the train and bus on which I had been riding.

After arriving back in Mountain View I found little interest by my townspeople in the war or in what I had been doing in it. But it was a two-way street. I not only did not want to talk about it but I wanted only to forget it. Indeed, my silence on my war experiences continued for many years and today I regret I did not tell my parents anything about it before they died.

There were many times when I thought about unburdening myself by talking to others about my experiences. But then visions would come into my mind about the hill at Nhpum Ga and the bodies of men and horses which lay there with the blow flies attacking them and the overwhelming stench that arose from the corpses which had lain there for so many days. I would think about the blood of both friends and enemies staining the waters at Walawbum. I would recall the diseases that afflicted all of us and the filth that arose from what appeared to be a mass case of dysentery among all the men of the Marauders. I would feel again the deep fears and anxiety that closed in on me during the days when I was lost in the jungle while we were climbing the dreaded Kumon Range in the monsoon deluges.

And most of all, strangely, I would think of the leeches and the virtual torrents of blood which arose every day and every night from the repulsive wounds they inflicted upon us.

I would think of only one or perhaps all of these things and then ask myself why in the world anyone would want to hear about them. Moreover, I did not find many people who were interested enough in the war to ask me what I had experienced in it.

But the days and the years have rolled by and suddenly there has been an outburst of interest in World War II. Today many people are expressing their interest in the war and in its vast significance in world history. One of them has been my daughter who forced me to look back upon the past and who persuaded me to write about my experiences. I also found a man who himself served in Burma in a less hazardous capacity and who volunteered to help me with this task.

Moreover, I have been persuaded to add the following two chapters to this book. They present information that is important because of its thundering impacts on the Burma war. Yet, to do it justice in the description presented to this point in my account of the war would have required lengthy digressions from the thread of events that has been described. Moreover, the additional material deserves separate treatment. One of these chapters will give the reader some engrossing insights into the controversial character and actions of General Stilwell in the Burma War. The other describes the wonderfully fascinating contributions of the Kachin hill people to the Allied cause.

THE VINEGAR IN VINEGAR JOE

General Joseph W. Stilwell's nickname of Vinegar Joe was well suited to him. No one knows who first tagged him with it, but undoubtedly it was someone who fell victim to his acerbic tongue, which he used on one and all indiscriminately. He employed it even in his many letters to his beloved wife which she nevertheless preserved for his posterity; and exceptionally few of the letters he mailed to her from India and Burma failed to contain at least one profane reference to Generalissimo and Madame Chiang Kai Shek, both of whom he held in utter contempt. Let it also be said that they held him in equally low esteem.

But their relationship didn't start out that way. In fact, Chief-of-Staff George C. Marshall appointed Stilwell as the commanding general in the CBI Theater precisely because he thought that Stilwell, who spoke Chinese quite fluently, would get along famously with China's ruling couple. And at first it seemed that Marshall's judgment was correct.

However, things changed rapidly when Stilwell and Chiang discovered they had opposing viewpoints on how the war should be waged. The judgment of history is that Stilwell usually held the correct view in their controversial relationship. In fact, Chiang constantly signaled his attitude that he couldn't care less about the war in Burma, and that his only interest lay in how much assistance he could get from America in his war against the Chinese communists. The only problem with his viewpoint was that the Communists, at that point in time were, not attacking him and, indeed, were assisting the Allies in the war against the Japanese. Moreover, his incompetence was revealed after the war when, even with all the weapons and supplies he received from the United States, and despite the fact that his forces greatly outnumbered those of the communists, he still managed to lose the civil war against them.

Consequently, most of the American soldiers who served under Stilwell admired the stand he was taking against Chiang. Moreover, we initially were impressed by the colorful and indomitable spirit we thought he displayed in his withdrawal from Burma early in the war. Everyone thought it was a valiant retreat despite the fact that such a phrase is an oxymoron. And it is true that he led a small band of survivors out of Burma in a 140-mile march through the jungles in the western part of the country. He was praised for bringing everyone out alive and for the fact that, at the age of 60 and not in the best of health, he led the column all the way at an accelerated pace.

But it was also true that Stilwell's little band did not have to cope with some of the tough conditions that plagued the Marauders in our march through Burma. Stilwell and his group of about 100 people had plenty of good food to eat, and they hiked along well-established trails where the threat from insect-bearing diseases was minimized. Indeed, no one has ever heard about any members of that band who came down with dysentery or malaria. And, even if they had, the column included in its members one Dr. Gordon Seagrave, the famed "Burma Surgeon," who would have been able to treat them immediately and effectively. The column encountered nothing but good weather on its flight out of Burma. Not a single casualty has ever been recorded with respect to that retreat. The half-dozen or so women nurses in the march survived it in very good shape, something they could not have done in an ordeal like the Marauders' experiences at Nhpum Ga or in other demanding challenges on the regiments drive through north Burma.

In other words, Stilwell's march out of Burma has been over-publicized, over-romanticized and certainly too much admired, particularly when compared with the challenges he meted out to the Marauders. Therefore, one certainly has to wonder if his negligence and sometimes his highly inimical treatment of the Marauders, not to mention his insistence on keeping their achievements under wraps, can be traced to his desire to emphasize only his own accomplishments, as doubtful as they were.

Another postscript to Stilwell's MacArthur-like tendency to dramatize a so-called heroic personal retreat is discovered when any genuine historian compares it with the experience of others. Some 900,000 people were killed when they tried to flee the country after the Japanese invasion of Burma. They included Burmese people, British troops, Indian soldiers and civilians, and two Chinese divisions led by Stilwell. To this day hundreds of skeletons of allied troops and civilians can still be seen where they fled along the trail across the Pitkai Mountains from Burma into Assam. Conversely, as noted above, not a single casualty or serious disease of any kind marked the -Stilwell retreat out of Burma.

Stilwell always maintained that the Chinese troops in that early part of the war fought valiantly against much larger Japanese forces, and, therefore, contended that they would perform even better if they were well trained. And sure enough the Chinese soldiers later trained by Americans proved to be a formidable force in the continuing war against the Japanese; but the command mistakes and inertia of their generals, as well as by their field grade officers, were atrocious. Witness their sad performance in the battle to take Myitkyina.

In any event, Stilwell insisted on training several divisions of Chinese for the Allied march back into Burma and his faith in them was justified in most of the missions in which they participated with the Marauders.

But there also was no question that he deliberately planned to use the small Marauders regiment to spearhead the attack. There also was no question that he agreed with his superiors in Washington when they predicted that the regiment would suffer up to an 85 per cent casualty rate. Yet, those close to him were not surprised when he rejected the Mountbatten offer to assign him a large British contingent to help him in the drive across North Burma and later also decided not to ask for British help in taking the town of Myitkyina after Japanese reinforcements had poured into the area.

The 'damn Limeys' he assailed so often in the letters to his wife, as well as in his communication with his staff officers, were absolute anathema to him. Moreover, like other generals, he wanted as much credit as possible to accrue to him, to his posterity and to his American forces. His conceit was enormous, and his altruism toward his soldiers was conspicuous only by its absence. Consequently, it quite apparently did not disturb his conscience when he expected and demanded that his own countrymen make the largest sacrifices in the war in the CBI Theater.

However, such sacrificial demands were not imposed upon himself and his son who served with him in the war. They never went into the front lines and Stilwell very seldom visited the Marauders at any point along their 800-mile peregrination in north Burma. Even after we captured the Myitkyina airstrip Stilwell spent only a short while there before hopping back into a plane to return to his rear area headquarters.

As a result of this callous negligence Stilwell never seemed to know anything about the difficulty of the Marauders' challenges. Far too many times his actions also revealed his lack of experience in actual military operations. His first experience in the command of combat forces did not occur until late in his life when he went to Burma.

But the biggest, the most severe, and the most despicable trait of the Stilwell character was exposed in his preoccupation with himself and his callous disregard of the challenges, achievements and the extreme hardships faced by his troops. Not only did he rarely, if ever, expose himself to enemy fire, but he displayed an almost complete indifference to the welfare of his soldiers who WERE involved in combat.

Consider the following: He never awarded a promotion to an officer or an enlisted man throughout the Marauders' campaign. He waited until after the capture of Myitkyina to award any decorations to either officers or enlisted men, and even then they were very few in number, approximately a half dozen if this writer's memory is correct. He must have been the first commander in American military history who yanked some of his soldiers out of hospitals to help in the campaign; something which occurred when he could have asked for and undoubtedly receive reinforcements from the British. Not only that, but the Mars Task Force which succeeded the Marauders marshaled more than a hundred thousand Americans, Chinese and Kachins for the campaign south from Myitkyina to Bhamo and Lashio in south central Burma. That this kind of strength was marshaled only after Stilwell was relieved of his command must tell us something about his incompetence.

Stillwell's complete disregard of his troops probably is dramatized best by the fact that he never authorized any kind of insignia nor even a name for the regiment he commanded. It was left to a newsman to suggest and popularize the name of the Marauders which, incidentally, refers to the men in the regiment and not to the regiment itself. In the records at the Stilwell headquarters the regiment always was designated as the 5307th Composite Unit (Provisional) and Stilwell never initiated or approved an insignia for the regiment. And it was left to someone in Washington to come up with the name of Galahad for the campaign that was waged by the Marauders, a rather romantic designation for the Burma war that was anything but that.

At least three-fourths of the books written about the Marauders have chastised rather than praised Stilwell. Let me quote from just a few:

From Lieutenant Charlton Ogburn's "The Marauders," one of the two most definitive books about the regiment: "In answer to a question of my father's as to what impression I had of Stilwell, I wrote that, to everyone I knew in the regiment, his name was as a red flag to a bull. ('I had him in my rifle sights,' said an enlisted man regretfully, speaking of the time at Myitkyina when Stilwell during an inspection had withdrawn to relieve himself. 'I coulda' squeezed one off and no one woulda' known it wasn't a Jap that got the son-of-abitch.') I (Ogburn) said that, while I had seen him (Stilwell) only once, he impressed me as a small man in a big job ... bloodless and utterly cold-hearted without a drop of human kindness."

From "Spearhead" by James E. T. Hopkins (a field surgeon with the regiment) who wrote the longest and by far the most detailed history of the Marauders and who previously had served in the South Pacific, I have excerpted the following passages:

"General Stilwell never visited the 5307th during our training period nor during our period of combat. (Except after the fall of the Myitkyina airstrip.) It is likely that, if our battalion surgeons had seen and examined him we would have been shocked by his general health.... he was almost totally blind in his left eye and the vision of his other eye required a very thick lens for correction. He died of a debilitating disease in 1946 soon after the war ended. In retrospect one has the right to condemn not only those two generals (the other being Merrill who suffered two heart attacks during the campaign) for accepting the great responsibility of commanding infantry troops in combat but also those who appointed them . . .

"On this day (May 20, 1944) General Stilwell wrote in his diary: 'Merrill passed by medicos. I let him go back to Myitkyina.' If any of the Marauders had known his thoughts it is likely that they would have asked him (Stilwell) why he didn't return to move among the men who had paid such a sacrifice under his command. They also would have wanted to ask him why he had promised to take them out of combat when the Myitkyina airfield was captured, and then not followed through or explain why he could not keep his promise. General Stilwell's plan to let the Marauders finish the job at Myitkyina can only lead me to believe that he had no knowledge of what they had been through, how few men remained and how, almost without exception, the men required hospital care for diagnosis, treatment and rehabilitation before returning to combat. His attitude must therefore have been due to lack of knowledge, total indifference to the health and survival of his troops, or early senility."

Finally, I present some excerpts from the book entitled "Galahad" which was written by Colonel Charles N. Hunter, the highly capable officer who actually commanded the Marauders most of the time because of the continued illness of Merrill. Indeed, if history were fair and just, our outfit would today be known as Hunter's Marauders instead of Merrill's Marauders. Hunter was in command at the crucial battle at Nhpum Ga and on the march to Myitkyina and during its subsequent capture. Hunter was so disgusted by Stilwell's incompetence and by his dereliction of duty that he wrote a long letter to Vinegar Joe telling him what he thought of him. Stilwell's response was to relieve Hunter of command and send him back to the states.

The following are only a few of the comments Hunter's book has to make about Stilwell:

Hunter wrote that, when told about the tough jungle terrain the Marauders would be marching through on the way to the regiment's first battle at Walawbum, Stilwell had both the ignorance and the audacity to say: "'If the terrain is like that how come I don't know about it.'"

When Stilwell insisted that the Marauders would have to finish the capture of Myitkyina town after the capture of the airstrip Hunter had this to say: "Had Stilwell planned deliberately to place himself and others in an embarrassing position prior to the rendering of his decision that Galahad (the Marauders) would finish the show I hardly know how he could have contrived a more impressive record. Stilwell believed that Merrill and Galahad could perform miracles."

On Stilwell's ability as a commanding general Hunter said: "Stilwell's disregard of the logistical requirements of warfare is, to me, incomprehensible. He apparently was able to justify to himself in some way going ahead with the execution of decisions that could, under no stretch of the imagination, be logistically supported. When informed in a conference one day that one of his proposed courses of action was logistically unsound he remarked caustically: 'Clive wasn't worried about logistics.' "

In summary of his views about Stilwell, Hunter had this to say: "Galahad Force (the Marauders) was the most beat upon, most misunderstood, most mishandled, most written about, most heroic and yet most un-rewarded regimental sized unit that participated in World War II. That it was expendable was understood from its inception. What was not understood, and has never been adequately explained, is why it was expended simply to bolster the ego of an erstwhile Theater commander such as Vinegar Joe Stilwell."

It also is important to understand that Hunter, despite his feelings toward Stilwell, did not write his book simply to make unsupported charges against him. Indeed, the publishers of Hunter's book quoted three responsible sources in support of Hunter's views: General A. C. Wedemeyer who succeeded Stilwell as CBI commander, Charles A. Grumich of the Associated Press Foreign Desk who covered the war in CBI, and James R. Shepley who covered the Asian action for Time Magazine.

Stilwell doubtless had his good points, like most leaders who hold a patriotic love for their country. General Marshall was one of his classmates at West Point, and throughout the war Marshall did not deviate from his admiration of Stilwell's genius as a strategist and tactician. And, indeed, Stilwell's strategic concept for the capture of Myitkyina was admirable, and so was his determination to achieve victory and end the Japanese terror. Unfortunately, however, he seemed incapable of gauging the costs of his campaign in Burma in terms of human lives, and especially the lives of his countrymen. To him victory not only was a desirable end, but it had to be achieved in the quickest manner possible, however costly it proved to be.

The greatest irony was the fact that the war would have been won by the allies without the help of the Marauders. The only requirement in Asia, as a result of the emphasis on the Pacific island strategy, was to fight holding actions against the Japanese and keep a large number of their soldiers occupied there. Regaining occupied territory in Burma and even in China was never a necessity.

Moreover, it was through the defensive action of British forces in south Burma, under the leadership of Mountbatten and General William J. Slim that made the major difference in Asia. Stilwell would have been better occupied by providing help to the British in that more strategic region than fighting an offensive war in the lightly populated jungles and mountains of north Burma. As it turned out the completion of the Ledo Road in north Burma had no significant effect in keeping China in the war. Transport by American airplanes continued to be the quickest and most effective manner of furnishing China with the weapons and supplies that Roosevelt and Churchill thought was necessary "in order to keep China in the war." Keep China in the war? Ironically, it was after the road had been completed that Japan launched one of its most successful offensives against China, sweeping through the eastern part of the country to capture highly strategic American air bases at Liuchow and Kweilin.

Moreover, a joint American-British effort in the south of Burma would later have enabled a massive joint offensive to the north which would have captured Lashio, Bhamo and Myitkyina with much greater ease than the monumental task faced by the unilateral American drive of the Marauders and Mars Task Force.

But Stilwell both refused help to the British in the south and rejected the offer of British help in the north. Instead, he insisted on a single-regiment offensive, bolstered by relatively few Chinese troops, in a brazen attempt to bolster his own ego with a dramatic but costly attack. Sadly, if he had waited just a few more weeks, he could have launched that offensive to open the entire length of the Ledo and Burma Roads with the 100,000-man force Mars Task Force which later succeeded the Marauders. But he couldn't wait. And when the Galahad campaign succeeded at a terrible cost he was able to pen a statement for posterity that read: 'This will burn the Limeys up.' Never mind that the Marauders had to suffer so much and sustain so many casualties. Stilwell, with his hatred of the British, had managed to 'burn the Limeys up.'

As far as is known he never had a favorable word to say about the Limeys' unflinching defense against the German Luftwaffe which, in the final analysis, had as much to do as anything with saving the world for democracy. Or, for that matter, did he ever praise or thank the British for their brilliant victory against the Japanese at Imphal in perhaps the largest and most significant land battle ever fought in Asia.

THE LOVELY KACHINS

They call themselves by one name and are known to the world by another; but whether Jingpaws or Kachins they have to be one of the planet's most interesting people.

Their exploits and way of life are so unique that people who have never been to Burma have a hard time believing the stories that American soldiers have told about them.

Indeed, most American wartime civilians never heard of the Kachins, and even fewer were aware of how much help they gave the Allied cause in Asia. This continues to be the case today and this writer would be remiss if he ended this book without a tribute to them.

Even the ancestral history of the Kachins is unusual. Their tribes originated in an area south of the Great Gobi Desert in Mongolia when Buta Khan, grandson of Genghis, was leading the famous "Golden Horde" of Mongols in their conquest of Asia and Eastern Europe in the 13th Century. But the Jingpaws, as they called themselves, were not Moslems like most of the followers of Genghis Khan, nor did they speak the same language. Indeed, the tongue they still use today did not have a written language or alphabet until Irish missionaries formulated one for them shortly before World War II began. The closest language to the one employed by the Kachins is said by linguists to be related to that which was spoken by the Turkish branch of the Altaic language family.

In their early years the Jingpaw tribes, like the Mongols, were known to be ferocious warriors who were good to their friends but fiercely retaliated against any cruelty their enemies displayed against them. Admittedly, this retaliation sometimes went to extremes as already has been described in this text. Kachins in World War II even mutilated the bodies of those whom they killed, inasmuch as they kept track of the numbers of enemies they had slain by cutting off the victims" ears. They then would put the ears in little containers and take them to American officers, telling them to divide the number of the auricular trophies by two in order to arrive at a formal body count in any particular battle. General Stilwell was so annoyed by this paganism and its unique kind of mathematics that he ordered his officers to make the Kachins stop the practice. But they had little luck in doing so.

The Kachins usually employed their highly effective ambush tactics when fighting the Japanese. However, they also participated in pitched battles, including one large one south of Myitkyina. The sum total of their effectiveness was belatedly described in a citation issued by Dwight D. Eisenhower several years after the war when he was president of the United States. Part of this citation reads as follows: "Under the most hazardous jungle conditions the Americans of Detachment No. 101 displayed extraordinary heroism in leading their coordinated battalions of 3,200 natives (Kachins) to complete victory against an overwhelmingly superior force. They met and routed 10,000 Japanese throughout an area of 10,000 square miles, killed 1,247 while sustaining losses of 37, demolished of captured 4 large dumps, destroyed enemy motor transports and inflicted extensive damages on communications and installations. The courage and fighting spirit displayed by the officers and men of Service Unit 101 in this successful offensive action against overwhelming enemy strength reflect the highest traditions of the armed forces of the Unieded States."

It should be noted and emphasized that only a relative handful of the combatants were American members of the 101 Detachment while the overwhelming number of it's soldiers were the Kachins. (Nearly all of the Americans were the officers and non-coms for the Detachment who had armed and led the Kachins.)

It is safe to say that the ties which bound the civilized Americans and the so-called uncivilized Kachins were as deep as any that have been noted in our country's military endeavors.

Despite their ferocity in combat, and the cruel revenge they took against their Japanese tormentors, the Kachins formed a friendship with the Americans that was probably deeper and more satisfying to our own soldiers than any which has occurred before or since in our country's wartime experience. Admittedly, this close relationship was hard to explain in view of the Kachins' cold-blooded mode of conducting warfare and the primitive way of life they followed in the jungles of Burma. Ray Peers, one of the two men who guided the detachment over its months of combat, perhaps gave the best explanation of how this relationship came about in the book "Behind Japanese Lines" by the late Richard Dunlop:

"The Americans represented the highest in industrialization, modernization, education and the like, whereas the Kachins were from the other end of the spectrum," Peers wrote. "They (the Kachins) were backward, primitive, and most of them were illiterate. Yet with all this difference the Americans and the Kachins had a great deal in common. There seemed to be some spark that attracted them to one another. This attraction was caused to a great extent by the character of the Kachins. They were courageous, resolute, dependable, honest and loyal. The only people who did not like them were their enemies and even they respected them."

I saw something else that also doubtless led to the mutual attraction of the Americans to the Kachins. Both peoples were highly extroverted and given to good-natured bantering of one another, something that was not so often seen among the British, Chinese and East Indian troops. Then, too, the Kachins, like the East Indians, doubtless found the actions of the kindhearted Americans to be a welcome change from the sometimes harsh treatment meted out to them by the British. Nevertheless, their valor was so great that even the British were able to lead them in a highly successful campaign near Fort Hertz in the extreme north of Burma.

Perhaps the most interesting characteristic of the Kachins is the vast contentment they find in their way of life. In an age of geometrical advances in technological conveniences and forms of recreation the Kachins have proven that they don't need them or want them. They maintain complete harmony with the nature from which their lives have arisen, in which they spend the rest of their lives, and to which they will return in the hours of their deaths.

Throughout past centuries most of them have been animists in their religion. The dictionary definition of animism is the belief that inanimate objects and natural phenomena are in possession of personal lives or souls. This was so true of Kachins during the time of World War II that the vast majority of them believed in nats. First, there were the "greater nats" like Mu, the nat of the heavens; Ga, the nat of the earth; Mbung, the nat of the wind; Bum, the nat of the sun, and Shata, the nat of the moon. Then there were any number of minor terrestrial nats, particularly the myriad spirits who inhabited every plant and animal in the jungle. Moreover, the Kachins did not deify the nats in a positive way but rather tried constantly to appease them so that they would not be punished by them.

Yet, despite their historical dedication to such spirits and beliefs, the Kachins took readily to Christianity. Thousands of them were converted to the faith, primarily to Catholicism brought into the country by priests, most of them Irish in their nationality. One of them, Father James Stuart, was a fabulous character who, early in the war, brought hundreds of Kachin women and children out of enemy held territory and into the safe hands of the Americans. Thereafter Father Stuart not only ministered to both Catholic and Protestant American soldiers but became a combat soldier of the first order. Indeed, he eventually was given an entire operational area to command for Detachment 101.

Several stories chronicled by various writers give the flavor of this heroic priest and his relationship with his beloved Kachins.

One of them began in the small village of Kajihtu while the Japanese reign of terror in the Hukawng Valley was still in progress. Father Stuart was leading a group of about 100 Kachin refugees toward the villages of Sumprabum and Napa well to the north of Myitkyina. When the group reached Napa in the North Burma foothills, the priest learned that a column of Japanese cavalry was heading down the road toward the village. Stuart decided to wait at the edge of the village for the column to reach the area. When it arrived Stuart saw that a major was riding his horse at the head of the column. The Japanese officer reined his steed to a stop when he saw the priest, raised his hand to halt the column, and then swung out of his saddle to confront Stuart.

"Are you Chinese?" Stuart blandly asked the major in English. "No, we are Japanese," the major replied, also in very good English. "Are you British?" the major asked and angrily spat on the ground.

"No, I am Irish," Stuart replied, and he then spat on the ground precisely where the major had expectorated.

The major glared at him in disbelief, drew his samurai sword, and with it scratched out a rough map of the United Kingdom in the dirt. Then he demanded that Stuart point out the location of Ireland on it. Stuart unerringly pointed to the correct position of his homeland on the map and he was home free, the Japanese in Burma hating the British and knowing the Irish had the same distaste for them.

Subsequently, the Japanese and Stuart's Kachins set up camps near each other and remained there for several days. But then a Japanese lieutenant, who had become friends with a Kachin boy, notified Stuart that the major now had decided that Stuart should be executed. Stuart fled into the jungle with some of the Kachins and headed back to the Colombian fathers' mission at Kaiihtu. There, Stuart was reunited with a Father MacAlindon with whom Stuart had been building the mission. With the Japanese still searching for Stuart the two priests decided to take to the trail and they headed toward British-occupied Fort Hertz near Burma's northern border with China. They had not gone far when they were stopped by another Japanese detachment; and again Stuart persuaded its officers to let them go because both of them were Irish. But some of the Japs, believing they were lying, followed the priests to a Kachin village where the two men bedded down for the night in the basha of the duwa (headman). Before they went to sleep the duwa gave them a box of hand grenades and two shotguns left behind by British officers when they had fled to Fort Hertz. He also warned the priests that Japanese soldiers had indeed been following them on the trail.

This disturbing news did not faze the two doughty fathers, who knew the Kachins would keep their location secret. They calmly went to sleep in the basha, but their slumber didn't last long. A few hours after they had bedded down the, Japanese soldiers entered the village and immediately lay siege to the basha. Awakened by their host the priests fired shotgun blasts through the roof and tossed the grenades through the basha's front entrance. Then they vaulted through a back window and fled into the surrounding jungle. Once in the wilderness the priests successfully eluded their pursuers. It required several days of tough movement through the brush but they finally arrived at Fort Hertz and safety. At Fort Hertz they were put on a plane and flown to India. But they hadn't been there long when a spokesman for Detachment 101 notified them that their services would be welcomed back in Burma to minister both to the Kachins and to Detachment soldiers. The Kachins, whom the priests loved so well, urgently needed them, the spokesman said.

Offered a reasonable sum of money to return to Burma, the priests accepted but used all of it in their post-war re-opening of the Colombian mission at Kajitu which they had founded to help the Kachins. And once back in Burma, they did much more than their share in the combat with the Japanese. Father Stuart, wearing a rakish Australian hat, also wore a belt to which both a pistol and a Kachin knife were attached. Photographs of him in this gear have appeared in several books about the Burma war with descriptions of how he successfully used his weapons in combat.

Perhaps the most treasured memory of the two priests concerns their return to their base from a Kachin festival at the village of Sumprabum. The jeep in which the two inebriated priests were riding suddenly started meandering all over the road. Said Father Stuart to Father MacAlindon: "Aren't you driving a bit erratically? Responded Father MacAlindon: "It is you who is doing the driving." Then, as Father Stuart recalled in his own report on the Burma war, he looked down on the steering wheel and the floorboard and discovered that, in his intoxicated condition, he was indeed the one who was operating the vehicle.

The communal life of the Kachins was as interesting as their military achievements. In some of the jungle villages the basha homes were situated on top of long, stilt-like posts. At first glance American soldiers concluded that this type of construction served to keep the bashas high enough that they would not be flooded out during the heavy monsoon season. And, indeed, the elevated homes probably had that advantage. But the Kachins themselves told us that this type of residence served mainly to protect them from nighttime prowling of jungle animals.

In some of the villages, there would be a longer and larger basha which served to meet community needs. One of them was to have a meeting place for the village elders who served in salang bawngs, organizations similar to American city councils. But these community buildings also served another important function. It was in them that Kachin young people prepared for marriage in a libertine fashion. They were members of a patriarchal society in which the seed of young men was prized and their fatherhood was a mandatory requirement to obtain eligibility for marriage. Hence the young men were regular visitors to the nla dap, the section of the community basha set aside for young people where they could satisfy their sexual desires, and at the same time establish their eligibility for marriage.

The young men, after selecting their prospective mates in the nla daps, had to become fathers in order to marry them and the young women had to help them achieve this status in order to obtain husbands. However, Westerners who would view this arrangement as immoral should take note of another feature of Kachin sexual mores during the wartime years. Once marriage took place there simply was no such thing as infidelity, and marriage became a lifelong status for all who took the wedding vows. Married men were severely punished if they were ever caught visiting a nla dap, and there was a time when they were even executed for such an infringement of Kachin moral standards.

All of which is in sharp contrast with the high divorce rate today in the United States that has resulted in deserted wives and children and broken families. Moreover, I assume, although I do not know, that Kachin societal rules have not changed in the past half century since the war ended.

I seldom saw a Kachin, man, woman or child, who did not radiate happiness and good cheer. Kachins talked volubly and smiled frequently. Indeed, it was such characteristics that endeared them to the Americans. On the other hand, the Americans quickly gave up any attempts to understand the Kachin language. There were double consonants in the language that had to be aspirated in order to arrive at the correct pronunciation. Moreover, some of the consonants sounded so much like one another that it was difficult to tell whether some words were being pronounced with a hard "g" or a "k," a "b" or a "p", a "d" or a "t".

The Kachin warriors were called hypenlas in their language and their mystical priests or wise men were identified as Jaiwas. The Americans at first were highly skeptical of the Jaiwas' mystical pronouncements and the sixth sense they claimed in detecting where the enemy Japs were located and what they were doing. But in a surprising number of incidents they turned out to be right.

My personal experience with the Kachins, as I have indicated earlier, was one for which I will always be grateful. I, of course, can never forget the Kachin who led me to safety when I was lost in the jungle. But there was hardly ever a day when Kachin guides did not show us the best way through the jungles or when they did not scout out Japanese patrols and warn us as to their locations.

It is in that connection that I will close with the stories of the second and third of the three Kachin boys I mentioned in the early part of this book, the first being Ndigu Ga who, the reader will recall, led the Marauders on the trail from Shingbyiyang to Walawbum. The second was Nau Yang Nau, a 14-year-old skinny lad, but one with a lot of typical Kachin guts and stamina. It was he who guided the Marauders' K Force column on the last night's drive toward the Myitkyina airstrip. It was important to surprise the Japanese troops at the strip and there was only one way to do it: Find one of those obscure mountain trails over the Kumon Range and follow it during the dark of night, a very difficult assignment.

Someone in the column had heard of Nau Yang Na's talents and brought him to the head of the column to lead it on its historic march to Mitch. And Nau Hyang Nau was doing very well when, shortly before midnight, he suddenly stopped and told an officer that a snake, undoubtedly one of the deadly Kraits, had bitten him. Immediate first aid was important because a Krait's bite usually resulted in death within 20 minutes.

But the only treatment available was to put the boy's foot into the cool wet mud in the area to reduce the swelling from the bite. While this was being done the men in the column were kept on hold while the fate of the Myitkyina attack depended upon the survival of young Nau.

But Colonel Hunter would have none of it. As fine an officer and as realistic as he was, he decided the fate of all his men and the importance of the regiment's mission mandated that the column had to keep moving. Consequently, he radioed the officers leading the column to resume their march. However, an army doctor at the scene, Dr. Bill McLaughlin, radioed back that the boy needed at least two hours of rest if he were to have any chance at all of surviving. Hunter responded with one of the most famous quotes of the Burma war. "Doc," Hunter replied, "he (the boy) must go on until he collapses. Too much depends upon him. I'll send up my horse. Put him on it and let's get going."

Despite the heavy odds against it the story had a happy ending. Nau Yang Nau survived, guided the Marauders unerringly toward Myitkyina, and the surprising of the Japanese troops was complete.

But not so happy is the story of Ngai Tawng whose life comprised one of the most poignant to come out of World War II, a story which was authenticated by author Richard Dunlop, a member of the 101 Detachment in whose arms the boy died. In his book "Behind Japanese Lines," Dunlop traced Ngai Tawng's life from the days of the Japanese terror in the Hukawng Valley.

Dunlop, now deceased, never gave Ngai Tawng's age, but apparently the boy was not yet in his teens when he was coming home from a quest in the jungle and heard the noise of the Japanese invasion of his village. He heard strange sounds that were made by Japanese soldiers, but he arrived in the village before they did. Soon after he arrived at the basha of his family, the Japs swept into the village, set fire to all of the bashas and herded the Kachins into the open area around them to perform the murders and the torture recommended to them by the Kachins' traditional enemies, the Shans. Ngai's mother and his sisters were killed, his brother was injured, and his father somehow escaped to fight the Japanese another day when Ngai Tawng was to join him. When his brother was shot and seriously wounded, Ngai Tawng tried to save him by ripping off some of his own clothing to use in trying to staunch the flow of blood from his wound. After several minutes the blood flow seemed to stop and Ngai Tawng picked up the old flintlock gun his brother had been using to fire at the Japs. (The gun had been given years ago to Ngai's father by the English commissioner for that district in Burma.)

But at that moment a Japanese soldier leaped into the basha and threw Ngai to the ground. The Japanese then set fire to the basha and dragged both Ngai and his brother outside where his brother was emasculated and then died. At the same time Ngai's cousin was also castrated and his penis and testicles were forced into his mouth.

Then it was Ngai's turn, but a strange and miraculous thing happened. The Japanese soldier who was to perform the despicable deed (believed to have been an officer with a good deal of authority in the invading force) suddenly held his knife in mid-air and loosened his grip on Ngai. Then he removed from his pocket a small leather container (similar to an American billfold) and drew from it a portrait of a smiling boy about Ngai's age who apparently was the officer's son. He then caressed Ngai's neck and the young boy, who could have withstood any kind of cruelty, broke into sobs at this unexpected kindness. Ngai later told American officers that the officer then slapped him sharply on the buttocks and the boy ran rapidly into the surrounding jungle. No gun was fired at him and Ngai soon found a good hiding place.

He rested there throughout the remainder of that day and the following night. The next day he started following a trail leading north and for the next 48 hours he survived, like any Kachin could, by eating fruits that grew in the jungle.

And then another miracle occurred. On the third day he stepped out of the jungle into a clearing and encountered Father Stuart and the refugees he was leading. Still later he was reunited with his father at one of the jungle bases created by Zhing Htaw Naw, a fabulous 'duwa' who became the Kachins' leader throughout Burma. Zhing Htaw Naw joined forces with Detachment 101 and he was a fervent and charismatic chieftain who led the Kachin Rangers all the way from Nawbum in north central Burma to Bhamo in the southeast part of the country.

Ngai Tawng quickly learned much of the English language and became a favorite of American soldiers wherever he came in contact with them. But it was in Dunlop that Ngai found his closest friend and mentor. This remained true all the way into the southeast part of Burma when the Mars Task Force succeeded the Marauders. The two men were in a party of Kachin rangers who were fighting along the Burma Road. One day, after they had met and routed a group of Japanese stragglers on the trail, Ngai, in fulfillment of his usual assignment, scouted ahead on the trail to be sure it was safe to move farther south on it. But in an unusual piece of very bad luck he was met and captured by some Shan villagers, Shans still being the bitterest enemies of the Kachins. It was incredibly tragic and ironic that the Shans treated him the same way they had successfully urged the Japanese to adopt in the Hukawng Valley terror. Like his brother before him, Ngai Tawng was castrated and then left for dead on the trail. And like his brother before him he died from the effects of the torture.

But he was still alive when Dunlop and his party reached the spot near the Shan village where the incident took place. Dunlop tried to stop the flow of blood from Ngai's wounds but it was to no avail.

"I do not want to live any more," he told Dunlop in English. And very quickly he passed from this world.

In writing about this tragedy Dunlop had this to say: "He died as a Kachin boy in the jungles, which is to say that he died bravely with a slight smile on his face and a last look of friendship in his eyes. His hand in mine grew limp and even to this day, decades later, I cannot write of this without feeling the tragedy of war."

I cannot think of a better declaration with which I should end this book.

THE END

Printed in the USA
CPSIA information can be obtained
at www.ICGtesting.com
JSHW012038250324
59897JS00014B/123

9 781630 269562